METAPHYSICS

JDV Philosophy Series - 5

METAPHYSICS
Philosophy of Be-ing for Today

Cyril Desbruslais SJ

Edited By
Kuruvilla Pandikattu SJ

Jnana-Deepa Vidyapeeth

&

Christian World Imprints

First Published in 2019 by

Jnana-Deepa Vidyapeeth
Ramwadi, Nagar Road, **Pune-411014**
jdvoffice@jdv.edu.in
www.jdv.edu.in
Phone: +91 20 41036111

&

Christian World Imprints
Christian Publishing & Books from India
H-12 Bali Nagar, **New Delhi-110015**
cwidelhi2017@gmail.com, info@christianworldimprints.com
www.ChristianWorldImprints.com
Phone: +91 11 25465925

ISBN: 978-93-5148-363-2

"Published with the help of the Institute of Missiology – Germany"

Printed in India.

CONTENTS

JDV PHILOSOPHY SERIES - 5

Since 1893 Jnana-Deepa Vidyapeeth has been pioneering philosophy discussion and debate inspired by prominent personalities like Richard De Smet, Jean de Marneffe, Salvino Azzopardi, Cyril Desbruslais, Noel Sheth, John Vattanky, etc. It has been in the forefront of promoting Indian philosophy and making philosophical thinking relevant for contemporary times. In its effort to reach out to like-minded scholars, JDV Philosophy Series is visualized as a catalyst for interdisciplinary thinking and contemporary exploration on social issues fostering holistic liberation, integral development and creative engagement.

JDV Philosophy Series (Books published so far)

1. Salvino Azzopardi: **Epistemology and Phenomenology of Religions** (2018)
2. Kuruvilla Pandikattu & Thomas Karimundackal (eds): **Melodies from the Flute** (2018)
3. Kurien Kunnumpuram: **Freedom and Joy** (2018)
4. Cyril Desbruslais SJ: **Postmodernity: An Indian Christian Philosophical Appraisal** (2019)
5. Cyril Desbruslais SJ: **Metaphysics: Philosophy of Be-ing for Today** (2019)

Books by Cyril Desbruslais SJ

1. Philosophy of Liberation: Revisiting Genuine Religious Experiences with Special Reference to Christianity
2. Postmodernity: An Indian Christian Philosophical Appraisal
3. Metaphysics: Philosophy of Be-ing for Today

EDITOR'S INTRODUCTION

What is reality? What does it mean to exist? How are we to be? What is it to be? How do we make sense of the things that we encounter every day? How do we understand the world and make sense of it? What is the nature of the world? Why is there something, rather than nothing? These are some of the bigger questions that we face in our lives?

This book is a humble attempt to approach these fundamental questions that relate us to the larger reality! These metaphysical issues are taken up in this book, with a view to making it easily accessible to ordinary readers.

Metaphysics as the basis of philosophy

The word *metaphysics* came to the vocabulary of classical Greek philosophy rather late. Plato knew of no such word and indeed, when it was first coined after an expression of an early editor of Aristotle, its meaning was extremely vague and general. The phrase *ta meta ta physika* was nothing but the collective and nondescript name given to the books of Aristotle that were placed after his treatise on Physics (Greek *meta* = after, *physika* = nature). This historical accident is not without significance for *meta* also has the connotations of "beyond" and whereas Aristotle's Physics could be summed up as a study of "nature" (the "physical" world), from the stand-point of the observable, which is the usual sand-point of the natural or physical sciences even today, metaphysics seeks to comprehend reality ("nature") at a deeper level and penetrate into its deeper depths, going beyond what mere sense-observation and experiment can reveal.

In this short book we give an introduction to metaphysics and deal with the what and how of it. Then we go on to study the transcendentals, which are qualities every being possesses because it is a being. Then we take up some general metaphysical issues like change, categories, causality and finally person.

It is hoped that this brief introductory study on metaphysics will be a launching pad to study other philosophical subjects deeply, since metaphysics provide us with the basis of philosophy.

The creative contribution of Desbruslais

It must be mentioned that Dr Cyril Desbsruslais, SJ, the author of this book is not primarily a metphysician. He is a versatile thinker and activist, who has specialised in Philosophy and English Literature. He is also fluent in French. He has a creative way of dealing with the concerns of the young people. Thus he has been primarily involved in liberating the young people and in proposing philosophical issues which will help them to be deeply human. Courses like "Philosophy of Liberation" and "Hunger and Poverty" were his popular ones. History of Philosophy, starting from Pre-Socratic Philosophers to Postmodernists has been his forte. He has also been taking courses on Philosophy of God, Philosophical Anthropology and Ethics.

This book on Metaphysics is based on his experience with these topics that he has taken up Metaphysics and Philosophy of Be-ing, discussed in this book. He has make it easily available to ordinariy readers. Basing himself on neo-Thomistic thinkers like Joseph Maréchal, Teilhard de Chardin and Karl Rahner, he has been able to formulate a creative, flexible and inclusive metaphysics, which is open to the world and affirming life in its totality.

As such, we appreciate greatly his contribution to creative and critical thinking relating to the Indian Church in particular and the larger issues of world in general. May this book help us to think globally, to live locally and commit ourselves totally, especially to the poor and the underprivileged!

PART ONE

THE BEGINNING

Chapter 1

What and Why

What metaphysics is all about and why we need metaphysics at all.

a. A forlorn hope?

Metaphysics! What is its nature, role and relevance? Immediately arises the question as to whether such an attempt is possible. And, in our technological age, any dream of "going beyond" the findings of sense-experience, out of which have emerged a variety of pragmatic inventions from space-craft to pocket computers, is understandably dismissed as precisely that: a foolish idle dream and nothing more.

The philosophy of being is "the effort to comprehend the universe not simply piecemeal or by fragments, but somehow as a whole." (F.H. Bradley)

"Explaining his Metaphysics to the nation – I wish he would explain his explanations." (Byron, Don Juan)

"Metaphysics is the finding of bad reasons for what we believe upon instinct; but to find these reasons is no less an instinct." (Bradley, Appearance & Reality)

"Die Welt die will betrogen sein...."

[The world, which wishes to be deceived ...] (Sebastian Brant)

In contrast to the clear and verifiable statements, measurements and laws of science, metaphysics seems to offer but a collection of high-flown words and phrases, shot through with vagueness and uncertainty. There is the amusing comparison of B. Hagspiel:[1] "A metaphysician is like a blind man in a dark room, looking for a black cat – which

1 *Smiles and Chuckles*, Illinois, Mission Press, 1952,1.

isn't there." And H.L. Mencken, the American journalist and satirist, wryly jibes,[2] "Metaphysics is almost always an attempt to prove the incredible by an appeal to the unintelligible." Or again, "the capacity of human beings to bore one another seems to be vastly greater than that of other animals. Some of their most esteemed inventions have no other apparent purpose, for example, the dinner party of more than two, the epic poem and the science of metaphysics."[3]

However, one may not be inclined to take Hagspiel and Mencken too seriously. After all, they are not philosophers in the strict sense of the word. And we don't go by a car mechanic's diagnosis of a terrible stomach-ache, nor do we set much store by a pianist's views on nuclear physics. But metaphysics culls some of its detractors from the ranks of serious philosophers, too! Language analysts are among the most rabid of the contemporary variety.

Rudolf Carnap, in his *Philosophy and Logical Syntax*[4] observes: "The danger lies in the deceptive character of metaphysics: it gives the illusion of knowledge without actually giving any knowledge." That, from an American. Then there is the Britisher, A.J. Ayer, for whom every metaphysical statement must be qualified as pure non-sense. He recognises, of course, that there is a time and place for everything – even non-sense. "If [an] author writes nonsense, it is because he considers it most suitable for bringing about the effects for which his writing is designed. The metaphysician, on the other hand, does not intend to write nonsense. He lapses into it being deceived by grammar, or through committing errors of reasoning."[5]

b. And yet...

Immanuel Kant, the father of critical philosophy and assuredly *the* Maker of the Modern Mind, recognises that metaphysics is the oldest of all disciplines, having already attained a hoary old age while physics and astronomy were still in their infancy. In fact, "in all [human beings], as soon as their reason has become ripe for speculation, there has always existed and will always continue to exist, some kind of metaphysics." This "metaphysics as a natural disposition", as he calls it, would doggedly continue the survive "even if all the rest [i.e. Scientific disciplines like physics and astronomy] were swallowed up in the abyss of an all-destroying barbarism."[6] And this is because it stems not from "an idle desire for extent and variety of knowledge" – is the sage of Königsberg suggesting that physics, astronomy and their ilk trace their origin to such roots? – "but proceeds impetuously, driven by an inward need, to

2 *Minority Report*, New York, Alfred K. Knopf, 1956, 238.

3 *Minority Report*, New York, Alfred K. Knopf, 1956, 56.

4 London, Trench and Trubner and Co., 1935, 20.

5 *Language, Truth and Logic*, London, V. Gollancz, 1951, 45.

6 *Critique of Pure Reason* B. 14ff.

question such as cannot be answered by empirical employment of reason, or by principles thence derived."[7]

> *Whereof we cannot speak, thereof we must be content to stammer!*

True, this "natural metaphysics", as Kant himself admits, has little to recommend it. Part opinion and part prejudice, highly tinged with dogmatism and illogical, it hardly merits serious attention – let alone the name of "discipline"! However, the very fact that we cannot help making metaphysics, however clumsily, should make us pause before we write off the whole enterprise. As Emerich Coreth[8] so rightly puts it, "Man is a metaphysical animal who cannot help asking the question of being." We should, therefore take a closer, second look at the views of those who are so eloquent on the impossibly of metaphysics. It could as well be due to questionable assumptions on their part or perhaps that many attempts to "metaphysicise" have started off on the wrong foot!

As a matter of fact, the objections of Carnap and Ayer fall into the first category mentioned above: they start out with a highly questionable presupposition, the famous "principle of verification" of logical positivism. As we may recall, according their – rather dogmatically assumed dictum – only empirically verifiable statements are true or, to put it their way, can be said to convey any sense at all. The assertions of metaphysics and all other "disciplines" which cannot be substantiated by empirical evidence are sheer non-sense. Leaving aside the gratuitous grounds for this bold and blind rule, suffice is it to point out that the very principle cannot be verified by empirical tests!

Along these lines runs the objection of thinkers who, enamoured by the clarity and precision of scientific language, want every branch of learning worthy of the name to be able to say their bit with that self-assured and precisely certain manner with which mathematicians, physicians an other scientists enunciate their various findings. "[W]hatever a man knows, whatever is not mere rambling and roaring that he has heard can be said in three words." Thus Kurnberger is quoted with approval by Ludwig Wittgenstein on the title page of his famous *Tractatus Logico-Philosophicus.*[9] And the closing sentence of that celebrated work is, expectedly, "Whereof we cannot speak, thereof we must remain silent." For such people, the struggling attempts of a metaphysician (for one), to put his insights down on paper and the whole absence of a self-assured "once-and-for-all" air about his pronouncements are sure signs that

---

7 *Critique of Pure Reason* B.21.

8 *Metaphysik,* Tyrolia, Innsbruck, 1961. See also his *Grundriss der Metaphysik.* Cf. Footnote 16.

9 Tran. & ed. D.F. Pears and B.F. McGuiness, London, Routledge and Kegan Paul, 1961. (First published in 1921.)

he is merely uttering "rambling and roaring", tales "full of sound and fury, signifying nothing."

Indeed, Wittgenstein's former ally, Bertrand Russell tried to give a metaphysical (I chose the word with full deliberation) foundation to the logical positivist position by putting forward his "picture theory of language." In his own words:

> A spoken language consists of a temporal series of events, a written sentence of a spatial series of bits of matter. Thus it is not surprising that language can represent the course of events in the physical world; it can, in fact, make a metaphysics of the physical world, preserving its structure in a more manageable form, and it can do this because it consists of physical events. But if there were such a world as the mystic postulates, it would have a structure different from that of language, and would therefore be incapable of being verbally described.[10]

In all fairness to both Wittgenstein and Russell, we must add that they both quickly gave up such a naïve understanding of language and words. Few – if any – would endorse their erstwhile tall claims on behalf of language. Nobody upholds the view that words are able to capture or encapsulate perfectly that which they point to. Linguistic terms serve only to *ap*-prehend, not *com*-prehend reality.[11]

Were we to agree with Wittgenstein and Russell when the former writes, "Everything that can be thought at all can be thought clearly. Everything that can be put into words can be put clearly," and understand by it that it would express exactly and totally al we have in mind, would have to remain silent whenever gripped by a powerful emotion such as grief, love, joy, thankfulness or sorrow. Aquinas seems the be more down to earth when he notes that we cannot avoid speaking about God (or, to paraphrase Heidegger, raising the question of being), "but when we do we can only babble."[12]

We babble because we are confronted with mystery and though we cannot remain silent before it, words cannot express our response adequately. And yet words we *must* utter for we have no other means of communication. And such deep experiences cry out for expression, albeit clumsily. Unexpressed responses to mystery are even more frustrating than stumbling, babbling outpourings. Whereof we cannot speak, thereof we must be content to stammer!

Precisely because metaphysics does not deal, as do the positive sciences, with the objective, detached data of the outside world, we cannot require it to speak with the same authority, exactitude and aplomb. Metaphysics raises questions of which we are a part. It tries to see how we ourselves fit into the

---

10 B. Russell, *An Outline of Philosophy*, London, Allen & Unwin, 1927, 46.

11 Cf. C. Desbruslais, *Rites and Rituals*, (mimeographed notes), JDV, Pune, 1986, 3.

12 Cf. ST I, 4 aa

> *The need for metaphysics endures. No one will shake it off. Metaphysics will be shunned by most people, always, because her path is not easy and no certain treasures lie at the end. Her poor cousins will be chosen in the preference, because they offer everything at no cost – a god to worship who has set us apart from the rest of creation and guarantees each an individual immortality and a will that is free to create destiny.*
> *People will always choose substitutes for metaphysics. Because of the indestructible need for her, they will accept anything, however tawdry, however absurd, as a surrogate. Yet it is only metaphysics that, while preserving one in the deepest ignorance, while delivering up not the smallest grain of knowledge of anything, will nevertheless give that which alone is worth holding to, repudiating whatever promises something better. For metaphysics promises wisdom, a wisdom sometimes inseparable from ignorance, but whose glow is nevertheless genuine, from itself, not borrowed, and no merely the reflection of our bright and selfish hopes.*[13]

whole scheme of things. We cannot study being, matter, sprit and so on with a distanced, uninvolved perspective any more than we can separate ourselves from ourselves! Metaphysical questions, then, like questions about love, the human person and life, cannot be expected to yield us guaranteed, absolute and once-and-for-all answers. To such questions we can only grope for responses, responses that throw a bit more light on the issue, responses that bring us one step further on the path to fuller understandings. This is not weakness of metaphysical matters; it is their strength. It is this that help to make everything more exciting, more interesting and more adventurous.

c. Metaphysics is inevitable

We are not satisfied by approaching life piecemeal or in small doses. We need to see it fully and see it whole. We need to sometimes raise questions about what other disciples take for granted. Whereas physics investigates the laws of motion and chemistry studies the structure of matter, we need to ask what is motion, what is matter, what is time? Nor are these merely academic issues, reserved for those who have nothing better to do, surely questions that a down-to-earth and busy person, or one who is struggling to eke out a living for himself and his family cannot afford the leisure to indulge in. As G.K. Chesterton

once said, "Nothing is more practical than a good theory." It is our implicit (often uncritical and naïve) answer to these questions that decide how, in the practical order, we act and think in the hurly burly of everyday. We need to take time out to examine our basic presuppositions, our assumed convictions, our blind acceptances. We should put them to the solid test of critical reflection

13 Richard Taylor, *Metaphysics*, Prentice-Hall, Inc, New Jersey, 1974, 8-9.

and personal analysis. Perhaps we have been unconsciously giving a rubber stamp to a lot of nonsense and unwittingly let these dogmatisms dictate our attitudes and our actions in the existential order! All this is what metaphysics is about. It's not a question of whether metaphysics is possible or not – for willy-nilly there cannot but be some kind of metaphysics – but **what** kind of metaphysics we wish to uphold: a random collection of irreconcilable dogmas and superstitions, culled from the latest social prejudices or something which is the fruit of critical endeavour and reflection? As we shall detail in the next chapter, our ability to transcend (that is, go beyond the immediate data of the senses) is as undeniable a part of our human experience as is our own existence. As Maréchal will show us, if we were not able to transcend we would not be able to make direct judgements at all (and we can't get away from making them!). Coreth and Rahner point out that to ask the very question, "is metaphysics possible?" is already to answer it in the affirmative; for we couldn't even pose the question without unconsciously affirming our capacity to transcend sense data. Furthermore, in that very act do we affirm all that is necessary to make metaphysics. More about all this in chapter 2.

d. Towards a definition of metaphysics

The most celebrated classical definition of metaphysics was given by Aristotle when he called metaphysics "**the science of being as being**."[14] This is a most ingenious definition, proceeding by genus and specific differences or, more precisely in terms of its material and formal objects (to keep the whole discussion with Aristotelian terminology.)

By the *material object* of a discipline we mean what preciously is the thing studied by that discipline. In everyday language we prefer to speak of the "subject" of a study. In the more precise vocabulary of philosophy, **subject** refers to the knower and **object** to the thing known or studied. The *formal object* of a discipline is the aspect or perspective from which it studies the particular material object. Now, "sciences are distinguished by the formal objects" for they all have the same material object, being. Where they differ is the aspect of being that they approach, the stand-point from which they view being. Thus mathematics studies being as quantified, aesthetics studies being as perceived to be beautiful. Metaphysics studies being (its material object) in its widest and deepest dimension, from the aspect of being itself (its formal object). To quote the words of Aristotle referred above, "There is a science which investigates being and the attributes which belong to its very nature." This is how classical and Thomistic thinkers view metaphysics.

My first difficulty with this definition is with calling metaphysics a *science*: inasmuch as metaphysics deals not with problems but mysteries, we cannot have

14 Cf. The opening sentence of his Book *Gamma of Metaphysics*, vol VIII in Ross' Edition.

a science of being, strictly speaking. A science, in the Aristotelian-Thomistic tradition is defined as *cognitio certa et evidents ex causis*, sure and evident knowledge (derived from a study) of causes – the four causes of Aristotelian philosophy. Since metaphysics is more "reflection trained on mystery" (as Gabriel Marcel would prefer) or "illumination of Being" (in Jasper's phrase), it cannot yield us that sure and evident knowledge from causes which is the hallmark of strict sciences like mathematics, physics, chemistry, astronomy and their ilk. As in any reflection trained on mystery, interpretation plays a large part. In the absence of methodologies that stress rational argumentation and irrefutable proofs there cannot be absolute certainty and binding evidence: we can fairly demand that only of a science that objectively analyses and dissects problems. Metaphysics cannot be a science in the strict sense. That is not its weakness. That is its grandeur – a grandeur which it shares with all the great treatises of philosophy! If we hastily conclude that all metaphysics is science we are looking for trouble. For thereby we invite comparison with the empirical sciences and then relegate it to some third rate position when we find it can't quite measure up to the standards of absoluteness and apodictic certitude that they seem to offer.

However, lest someone jump to the other extreme and infer that metaphysics is an irresponsible, irrational and whimsical flight of fancy according to our favourite prejudices and preferences, let us emphasise that it is an **investigation**, an **enquiry** that is **critical** and **reflective** and its findings and interpretations being from experience and are to ever be tested in the light of the accumulated experience of history as well as our own personal lives. In other words, it tries to approximate those other responsible virtues of the sciences – consistency, clarity, criticalness and creative insight. Dogmatism, haphazardness, internal contradictions and clumsiness, all these are as much excluded from metaphysics as from the empirical disciplines.

A more contemporary definition of metaphysics can be sought in the words of the existentialist philosopher, Martin Heidegger: "An enquiry into the Being of beings." This phrase throws into relief my dissatisfaction with the latter part of Aristotle's definition. In most languages, "being" (or its equivalent) has to function both as a noun and a verb; it can refer to things that be or to the activity of be-ing. Invariably it ends up being viewed as a noun and its verbal sense is tacitly accepted as a very inactive type of inactivity, a mere static fact (rather than a dynamic act), the lowest and least in the scale of "doing-words". Metaphysics has thus come to be characterised, as Jaspers and Heidegger remind us, by a forgetfulness of **Being**, that is of "being" in the verbal sense. Most metaphysicians after some polite noises in its direction, leave aside the mystery of Be-ing (verbal sense) and settle their sights on existents, things that be. These are studied in a detached, objective way, as "things outside there" and metaphysics is well on its way to (try and!) become another science along with physics and chemistry and so on. But shouldn't metaphysics go into the depth-dimension of existents (being: noun sense), which is their very act of existence, their "to-be" which enable them to be beings at all! To distinguish the verbal sense of being from the nominal (noun) sense, Heidegger capitalised the former. We might do well to adopt a similar procedure. So I would like to point out that when I write "Being", I am not speaking of God who is another example of being. I know many people would not be happy that God and creatures are being apparently put on the same plane as so many instances of beings, but I hope people will understand the context within which I am speaking and not worry to make out a case to the effect that I am plain and simply putting God and creatures on the same level. As it will soon be obvious, I uphold the analogical notion of being and will show that the beings of this world are ontological participation in God, who is the supreme being, the primary analogate of the usage of the word.

Heidegger is, of course, realistic enough to recognise that we have no direct access to Being: as far as we are concerned, we can only encounter Being in and through beings which make it manifest to us. Hence his "enquiry into the Being of beings". This is all very well, but is it existential enough? What concerns us in the real life situation of beings – human beings and other beings? Metaphysics is relevant inasmuch as it throws light upon the existential situation of people and the world. What is the value of an enquiry into a will-o'-the-wisp, in itself, except in so far as it enables us to come to grips with the concrete, existential beings of our daily experience and helps us to build up healthy attitudes of commitment and care towards them? Of course, a good deal of this will also depend on our understanding of, and attitude to, Being. But an enquiry into Being is not, cannot be, for us an end in itself. Hence, I arrive at the following definition of metaphysics: **a critical reflective enquiry into the mystery of Being and of beings**. The former is the means and the latter is the end of the enquiry.

After two introductory chapters, then, our treatise will be broken up into two parts. In the first we will enquire into the nature of beings and, since the beings of our concrete experience are all tangible in some way or the other, we will devote the lion's share of this to a plumbing into the depths of what is traditionally called "material" being. This, of course, will entail an attempt to clarify exactly what we mean when we are talking about "matter" and "spirit". We all use these words and so we have at least some vague understanding of what they mean. We shall try to bare, or make explicit, what is implied in such common usage. Common usage is, as we all know, not a very reliable guide in precising philosophical terminology. But it can be a useful starting-point. It invariably enshrines the wisdom of the ages and, if it had been roughly handled with the passing of time (or decked in not a few prejudices and presuppositions), then the right course would be to seek the kernel of insightful knowledge enshrined therein. Critical reflection has often a lot to learn from common usage, at least indirectly.

In the latter part, we shall seek to penetrate into the heart of Being, as Jaspers and Heidegger have advised us. Our approach, then, will be to begin with what is immediately and directly accessible and pass thence to what lies behind at a deeper level and which the former seems to point towards. This is the approach of hermeneutical phenomenology.

e. Approaches to beings and Being

Generalisations tend to exaggerate. But if they do, let us not forget that exaggerations underscore a vein of truth. It is with this caveat that I introduce my generalisation about "Indian" versus "Western" approaches to metaphysics. We all know perfectly well that Eastern and Western thinkers do not proclaim their respective views in polyphonic chorus. Still there are some, more or less, common emphases, perspectives and preoccupations that enter into their approaches, procedures and conclusions. Of course there are exceptions. But don't these only serve to "prove the rule", as the old saying goes?

This cautionary paragraph was necessary to preface my observation that whereas Western metaphysicians tend to start with reflection of what we might call "the external world", "objective reality" or "being under its transcendent aspect", Indian (predominantly classical Hindu) thought, focuses its attention on the self, the ego, being in its immanent aspect. A brief introduction to the Indian metaphysical emphasis is given in the last section.[15] Some recent Western thinkers have also tried to integrate the more "interior approach" of the Indians sages into their metaphysical systems. Apart from Heidegger there is the work of Emerich Coreth, *Metaphysics*[16] and that fine study of Scheur's philosophical synthesis by Daniel Shine, *An Interior Metaphysics*.[17] My own line of study will be inspired by Joseph Maréchal and his "intellectual dynamism" method of transcendental analysis of direct judgement. His five *cahiers* (especially the last) entitled *Le point de départ de la métaphysique*[18] have opened up new vistas for many Western thinkers who had felt the need to integrate the complementary "ways" of Western and Indian metaphysics.

---

15 For those interested in an Indian approach to metaphysics, John Chethimattam's *Consciousness and Reality* is an excellent introduction. Bangalore, Dharmaram College, 1967. We shall make use of this book towards the end of this treatise.

16 (ed.) Joseph Donceel, Herder and Herder, 1968. He has published a revised summary of his metaphysics entitled: *Grundriss der Metaphysik*, Tyrolia, Innsbruck, 1994. It gives an updated exposition of his matured views on metaphysics.

17 Massachusetts, Weston College, 1966.

18 Paris, Desclée, 1949.

Chapter 2

How?

How do we set about doing metaphysics?

We have, in our first chapter, tried to show what metaphysics is and why we need metaphysics. We saw that metaphysics "as a natural disposition" is a given fact of our experience. We cannot discuss whether it is possible or not, whether it exists or not, any more than we can argue as to whether we exist or not! In fact, even to raise the issue of our own existence is already to embark upon "metaphysics as a natural disposition". But is it possible to elaborate a conscious, critico-reflective, coherent and consistent body of insights into an over-arching vision of reality as such? It is in this sense of a *Weltanschauung*, as the Germans call it – and only in this sense – can we speak of metaphysics as a strict science. How do we set about doing this? What is the method to use? In other words, we are busy with the "how" of metaphysics.

a. The starting-point

Intimately bound up with the issue of the "how" of metaphysics is the question of the "where", that is where to start. The methods of the starting-point of metaphysics are closely inter-related. Let us first list the requisite qualities for these and then we shall cast about for what fits the bill.

In the first place, the starting points should be as solid and certain as possible: after all, if we are going to build our whole metaphysics on a foundation of sand, we aren't going to raise a very dependable edifice. This becomes all the more a matter to be reckoned with if we recall that metaphysics is meant to provide the basis and bedrock for other disciplines, giving a ground to all that they take for granted.

Secondly, it should not be some recondite, erudite or esoteric procedure or sphere of reality to which, few, if any, have access. Mystical experiences and the like are all very well and the genuine variety, no doubt, gives us inspiring and illuminating insights into the depths of reality. But, apart from the fact that it is not easy to differentiate between illusion and the authentic stuff, most of us lesser mortals do not know how to do such things and metaphysics and its conclusions should be something that everyone should be able to work for ourselves.

Finally, our starting point should put us in contact with the world around us, not just lock us up in ourselves. Descartes' chilling words at the beginning of *Meditations III* are, as far as I am concerned, a good lesson in how *not* to philosophise.

> I will now close my eyes, I will stop my ears, I will turn away my senses from their objects, I will even efface from my consciousness all the images of corporeal things; or at least, because this can hardly be accomplished, I will converse only with myself, and closely examining my nature, I will endeavour to obtain by degrees a more intimate and familiar knowledge of myself.

Our embodiedness, whether we like it or not, roots us in this tangible world. Hence, we cannot understand ourselves by isolating ourselves form our situation, which is as much part of ourselves as our own personal identity. Trying to comprehend human beings after uprooting them from the world (or trying to do so), is like trying to study the life of fish after taking them out of water so as to observe their behaviour on a drawing board!

Besides all this, we need a starting point that provides a fruitful meeting-point between human beings, the *subject* and the world, their *situation*. Descartes' starting-point, the *cogito*, left out of the picture not only the external world but also our embodiedness. No wonder he ended up identifying himself with his mind and, apart from the problem of the bridge (how does one bridge the gap between the self and the external object?), he couldn't quite figure out how he (his mind) was related to the body at all. Of course, the whole difficulty stemmed from the fact that *cogito* is not a true starting-point for metaphysics at all. It presupposes other elements and so is no valid foundation. In the first place, "I think" is an abstraction. No one merely "thinks" he thinks this or that concrete thought about this or that particular reality. And, even before that, before he can think of a particular person or thing, he must sensually perceive that reality – at least indirectly. If we make the Cartesian blunder of starting with an abstraction, we will be left with an abstraction and hard put to get back to concrete reality. Over and above these difficulties, the Cartesian *cogito* labours with other problems, as Heidegger points out in *Being and Time*: the father of rationalism quite overlooks the mode of being (*die Seinsart*) of his *res cogitans*, hastily assuming its substantial nature.

Emerich Coreth, very insightfully points out that the question that Kant posed himself in his *Critique of Pure Reason*, is unthematically answered in the very act of formulating the query. That question is formulated as: "is metaphysics possible?" Now, if Kant hadn't taken such a static view of human knowledge, he might have realised that the very dynamism of knowledge that is implied in stating such a question contains within itself all that is required to give an affirmative answer. The "pre-understanding" of the question conveys the ingredients of a positive reply. The original German edition of this Jesuit professor of philosophy at the university of Innbsruck, Austria, *Metaphysik*, was first published in 1961. There is an excellent (abridged) translation by Joseph Donceel, with an appreciative appraisal by Bernard Lonergan. As Emerich Coreth's endeavour closely approximates that of Maréchal, I will append an explanatory and critical comment on his work after I have detailed the approach of the Belgian.

b. The DIRECT JUDGEMENT as starting point[1]

For Kant, a judgement was (epistemologically speaking) a mere mental union of subject and predicate – the linking together of two concepts in our mind. In the Thomistic tradition to which Maréchal belongs, that is but a necessary stage in the formation of a true and valid judgement. The actual judgement is made only when one affirms that the mental linkage of Subject and Predicate is verified in some existential reality. I other words, what constitutes a judgement is not some static intra-mental fact, but a dynamic extra-mental act which puts us intimately in touch with the world of our experience. More precisely, what we call direct judgement is the affirmation or denial that something concretely exists. It is called "direct" because such an affirmation is made directly and immediately, that is to say, it is not the conclusion one arrives at on the basis of some other knowledge: it is straightaway perceived or intuited. Direct judgements then are rooted in direct or immediate sense experience. Such would be statements like, "This is a table" or "That is not a dog." Other affirmations or denials like, "God exists" or "There is no such thing as a soul" are not based on direct perception. They are conclusions at which we arrive after having interpreted some other knowledge which we have derived directly from experience. We might, comparatively, call them "indirect" judgements.

We may pause for a moment to note that our starting point is not an abstraction as Descartes' was. It is an **action**, an activity which we seize upon and delve into while it is still going on. It is **concrete** and forms a vital link

1 See also another version of the same argument in my *Philosophy of the Human Person*, JDV, 1997.

between us and the world around us. It effects a vital subject-object link and, indeed, establishes a subject and an object at one and the same moment, through one and the same act, from what previously could have been designated as a mere ego and a mere thing, respectively. And it is **immediate**: it doesn't presuppose any previous activity or experience. Finally, it is a **metaphysical fact**: one can be absolutely sure of its reality. If one were to deny the direct judgement, one would be contradicting oneself for one could only do so while making another direct judgement. It would be as foolish and self-contradictory as denying one's own existence. Both acts implicitly affirm what they explicitly deny.

The direct judgement, in brief, is an ideal starting-point. Let us now proceed to show that it contains within itself all that we need to build up a valid metaphysics.

It might not be out of place, at this juncture, to show how Coreth's approach (with the starting point as question) ties in with Maréchal's. The very question, "is metaphysics possible?" can be shown to be founded on the implicit direct judgement that something exists. Thence we may come back to the more basic and originally starting-point of Maréchal.

c. Our methodology: transcendental analysis

Here again we borrow a page from Kant, grateful to Maréchal having opened our eyes to this fecund insight from the work of the great Sage of Königsberg. And once again we cannot suppress a sigh of disappointment over the fact that Kant's static understanding of the dynamic act of knowledge blinded him to the inestimable worth of the method he had himself discovered.

The method of metaphysics cannot proceed along the lines of traditional deduction, which starts with some universal premises. If metaphysics is to be the basis of all other disciplines, it can't borrow unjustified general principles form anywhere else. Nor will induction help in itself. Besides, both these methods stand in prior need of justification before they can be appropriated as tools for action. All what is left to us is to start with some undeniable fact (like the direct judgement), analyse it critically and reflectively and seek to uncover all it implies. Obviously, whatever can be shown to be a necessary pre-condition for the existence of something which cannot be denied, must also be admitted as that which cannot be denied. And that is precisely what we do in transcendental analysis (variously called transcendental reflection and transcendental deduction). The term "transcendental" implies a "going beyond". In such a deduction or analysis or reflection, we aim at going beyond the particularities of a given direct judgement to discover what are the pre-requisites for any direct judgement to take place at all. I prefer the name transcendental analysis as it is more to the point and less open to misunderstanding and confusion.

d. Preliminary discovery: direct judgement is a movement

This initial finding is significant and it corrects the Kantian lacuna. All our knowledge is based on direct judgement, fundamentally. If direct judgement is a dynamic act, a movement, a process, then knowledge is no mere passive reception of data from the outside and subsuming these under various a priori forms and categories, as Kant had opined. Knowledge is the result of a drive from within us, we know because we want to know. We are not merely "open to the world" (*Weltoffenheit*, as Pannenberg would say). We are positively driven out of ourselves to the world around us. That this is the case is borne out, first of all, by the data of our own experience. We want to know; no one is content to remain in a state of ignorance. Indeed, obtaining knowledge is not an easy job: we often have to struggle against severe odds to get at the truth and very often we fall into error. But this doesn't daunt us. We throw ourselves back into the battle and are not satisfied until we have found it. The whole of Indian philosophy, which sums up human striving as a relentless effort to pass from *avidya* (ignorance) to *vidya* (knowledge), confirms this. Again, the traditional Thomistic recognition of the various states of the mind on the way to the attainment of knowledge is an implicit recognition that knowledge is a very definite process, a movement from a state of not-knowing to the triumph of knowing. We begin with **nescience** (not knowing what we are not really supposed to know by our particular profession or way of life: this is inculpable), or **ignorance** (not knowing what we, by our profession or way of life are supposed to know: this is culpable). Then there comes **doubt**, a fluctuation of the mind between two extremes of a stance. **Suspicion** implies a definite inclination or bias in favour of one view, rather than another; however, this bias has no basis. It could be an insightful and uncanny intuition that accounts for it, a blind prejudice might be its ground just as well. Next there is **opinion** when some clear reason in favour of one's inclination begins to emerge, but this reason is not at all conclusive and one recognises that he could be in error due to insufficient evidence. Finally, there is **certitude** where the mind comes to rest and makes a clear and firm assent to a particular stance and has no fear of error as the evidence in favour of one's position is quite irrefutable and solid. Now, the very fact that we can distinguish in our consciousness between these various moments, is a clear indication that we come to know as the result of a definite quest, a movement that drives us from within to the world without. A closing clinching argument is provided by our own experience of inattentiveness! We all know times when we have "tuned off" from a lecture or a TV programme. The sound or light waves have been impinging on our various sense organs but we do not record any knowledge of what was going on. Now, if knowledge were a purely passive affair, a mere reception of sense data, it would be absolutely impossible for us not to pay attention. This just brings out the fact that knowledge is constituted not by the mere fact of passively receiving sense data but by the active going out and integration of it into one's life. Knowledge, clearly, is a dynamic act, a process, a movement.

e. Does all knowledge aim at a common ultimate goal?

That knowledge is a movement is something which, I hope, is quite clear to all of us. The next logical question that arises is assuredly the query as to whether this movement of knowledge has an overall definite goal or is it just a general centrifugal movement from us in any direction. Obviously enough, the immediate and proximate goals of my intellectual endeavour are various: the particular concrete objects that I explicitly affirm when I make my direct judgements. But is there some overall common ultimate goal that lies behind the existential affirmations of chairs, tables, human beings and what not that I keep making in my daily life? If we may anticipate things a little bit, we can say, "yes-there is"!: the Unlimited Existence. In other words, though I may be consciously and explicitly reaching out to the affirmation of a cat or a pen through a direct judgement, I am unconsciously and ultimately striving to affirm the existence of the Unlimited Being (or Existence); indeed, it is because of this prior and ultimate orientation that I actually affirm the more proximate and concrete things at all!

f. The common ultimate goal of all my knowledge is the UNLIMTED BEING

To show that this is the case, we must go a bit more deeply into what's "at work" in our explicit affirmations by way of direct judgements. Now, all direct judgements take the form, "This is (or is not) an X." In other words, I affirm two dimensions: that something is (or exists) and that it is **such** (that is, a table, a chair or whatever). In metaphysical language we say that we are affirming its essence (**what** it is) and existence (that it **is**). Now let's look a bit closely at each of these elements.

As regards the essence, we note that it is a limited and self-limiting dimension. To be a cat or a dog or even a human being is, indeed, a perfection, a positive quality. But it is also a limitation. If one were a cat or a dog, that prevented one from being a horse or a mango – in short, from being non-cat or non-dog. Now, non-cat and non-dog are no mere negations. Lots of positive things come under the scope of non-cat and non-dog – horse, human being and cow, for instance. Essence, then, is a limitation (besides being a positive quality or perfection). And it is self-limiting. The very catness of a cat prevents it from being a dog or a horse. As we said, essence is encountered by me as a limitation that is self-limiting.

Now let's turn to a consideration of existence. Existence is a pure perfection. It doesn't imply any limitation or imperfection. Existence is opposed to non-existence. Non-existence is nothing. It is not like non-cat or non-dog which implies some positive qualities. But, though existence is, in itself, a pure and unlimited perfection, we actually encounter it only in a limited state – as, for instance, in the existence of **this** table as opposed to the existence of **that** table or my own existence or the existence of a particular chair. Thus, though the existence that I experience and explicitly affirm in direct judgements is limited, it is not self-limiting. Unlike essence, existence doesn't limit itself (as we saw above). In itself it is unlimited: it is limited by something else, something other than itself – to be precise, by essence.

What does all this mean? It means that the dynamism of my intellect, in and through the direct judgement, is ultimately tending towards the unlimited existence. After all, when a movement experiences a limit as such, that is an obvious indication that it is tending beyond the limit. What acts as a limit to the movement of intellectual striving in me is the fact that I encounter existence (unlimited in itself) as limited. Hence I am tending, not to the affirmation of merely a "bigger and better" dose of existence (for inasmuch as that would still be limited, it would still show up as a limit to my intellectual dynamism) but towards an encounter with the unlimited existence. Unlimited Existence, then, is the ultimate goal of my intellectual dynamism, the implicit final end of my intellectual dynamism which *proximately* and explicitly finds its immediate end in the affirmation of particular concrete realities.

g. But is this UNLIMTED EXISTENCE real?

Kant recognises that our mind is so made that in affirming the direct judgements of our perception we are ultimately tending towards the affirmation of the UNLIMTED EXISTENCE. But for him this "totality of being" is only a "transcendental ideal". Our mind is so constituted that it can only affirm concrete things because it is ultimately oriented towards the unlimited. But *lex mentis non est lex mentis*, the laws of the mind are not the laws of reality. Just because our mind is so made that it functions on a kind of presupposition that here is an unlimited existence behind all that I affirm, it does not mean that in reality, there is an unlimited existence that somehow grounds all else that is!

Maréchal's rejoinder is that such is precisely the case. *Lex mentis est lex entis*, the law of the mind is the law of being! We can proceed to show that the unlimited is no mere empty ideal, a kind of epistemological, subjective necessity for our mind and something for which there is not necessarily anything corresponding in reality and this is done in the following way.

Maréchal's procedure is to point out that if we admit the reality of the world around is, which is the object of the affirmations we make through direct judgement, then we must admit – with even greater assurance – the reality of the unlimited existence. After all, as proximate and partial ends of my direct judgement, they derive their status and reality from the ultimate and total end of my intellectual dynamism (the unlimited being). If the former are real, all the more reason as to why the latter – in whom they room and ground their reality – should be real too.

But why should we grant the reality of the external world? After all, some philosophers (Buddhists, some schools of idealism and Hindu philosophy) have denied it. True, some have merely meant that *compared to the Absolute*, i.e., relatively, it is unreal. But others have been quite uncompromising in their avowal of its illusory and fundamentally vacuous nature. However, Maréchal points out, there is more reason to believe in its reality than its non-reality. And it is surely a good scientific attitude to opt for a theory that has more basis in its favour rather than support one which has less points for it. What are the points in favour of the reality of the external world? First and foremost our very natural disposition, supported by the spontaneous urging of our sense and intellect. Against its reality stands only a particular speculative approach which flies in the face of our most natural and spontaneous convictions, preferring to attach more weight to a particular speculative and theoretical viewpoint, which is based on one possible approach to being – an approach which lands one in conclusions which are not warranted by our everyday experience (even if we believe that the world is metaphysically speaking, unreal, we have to act and behave in response to it *as if* it were real!).

Another angle of approach, which equally assures us of the reality of the UNLIMTED EXISTENCE (or Being), starts off from undeniable fact that it is **existentially possible**. We saw that the UNLIMTED BEING is a necessary pre-condition for the undeniable activity of direct judgement. In other words, we have derived its possibility not from the mere analysis of what a particular concept entails, showing that the notion of it contains no inherent contradiction – which would be tantamount to showing it is **conceptually** (or essentially) **possible**, whence we would not conclude to its existential reality! However, with the direct judgement we are already in the existential order, inasmuch as we are busy with an activity, a movement, a dynamic process and not just a mental construct.

Now a thing may be existentially possible in three ways. One is by the actual fact of its existence, here and now. I exist, therefore I am possible. Or it could be existentially possible in the sense that it did actually exist in the past, but no longer exists now. We can conclude to that by showing it to have been the necessary precondition for the existence of something in the present whose existence is admitted. Thus, from my existence we can conclude to the existential possibility of my father (who happens to be dead and so doesn't actually exist now – at least, not in the sense that you and I exist). Or a thing my be existentially possible in the future, in the sense that though it does not actually exist yet, all that is required for its existence is ready and present: it just has to be assembled. Such would be the case of the table which a carpenter wishes to make, if all the wood, the nails and whatever else by way of material and tools are there, just waiting for the carpenter to get to work on them.

God, the Unlimted Being, does not emerge as the superstructure of an intellectual activity. He is discovered as the goal of my very depths, as that which urges me to activity from my very depths. He is active in the very depths of my being.

Now, if the UNLIMTED BEING is existentially possible, it must exist. It cannot be a being that actually existed in the past but no longer exists or is not yet actually in existence but awaits some efficient case to put it together. As UNLIMTED BEING, if it is existentially possible, it must exist actually now for there is nothing other than itself to prevent its existence to be realised. Other beings which are limited may be existentially possible but may not necessarily exist here and now (my father or the table the carpenter has yet to assemble).

Finally, one can also attempt to indicate the actuality of the UNLIMTED BEING by pointing out that it operates on my activity as an unconsciously sought goal. Hence it cannot be an illusory or mentally fabricated end for, in that case, I would be seeking it with full awareness.

Each of these three independent approaches leads to the same conclusion; they all converge towards the same terminus – the actuality of the UNLIMTED BEING or Existence.

h. Heidegger's purpose achieved!

Martin Heidegger called for an enquiry into the Being of beings. And we know what he meant by that. But isn't this precisely what Maréchal has inaugurated? We started with the concrete beings of our everyday life. We followed through into its deepest depths the activity of direct judgement which affirms such a being. Then we made a transcendental analysis of what goes on in the dynamic activity of that affirmation, following through our encounter with the Being of that being. And we found, through that analysis, that our intellectual dynamism is an activity that is but triggered off by our encounter with the Being of beings but is ultimately oriented towards the affirmation of the Being of Being. Maréchal has brought us, as far as it is possible for us, in touch with that elusive Being which should be the ultimate concern of metaphysics!

In the latter part of this treatise, we shall attempt to penetrate even deeper into the heart of Being. For now, we shall pause and see what we can glean about the nature of those manifestations of Being to which we have access, beings, to be more precise, material beings: the beings that we can sensibly perceive in the world that surrounds us. But, before we do that it might be good to draw our attention to some of the the basic metaphysical truths that are exercised by us in the activity of direct judgement, truths which are at the basis of all knowledge and on which every discipline is constructed. And, inasmuch as they are necessarily pre-supposed for the undeniable activity of direct judgement, their own objective validity is assured.

i. Quite a mixed bag!

Maréchal, as we know, would hesitate to call any of these a "proof" for God's existence or the principle of causality or whatever. After all, in a rational proof, we use a process of logical deduction to conclude to the existence of some truth whose validity was actually unknown to us, neither implicitly nor explicitly. Our exploration of the implications of direct judgement has not proceeded along the lines of logical argumentation and deduction: on the other hand, we have made a transcendental analysis of the activity of direct judgement, only to lay bare what we have been implicitly affirming in and through that process itself. In other words, we are merely making explicit what we had known all along in an implicit manner. Thus he prefers to call what we are doing a "demonstration", a "calling-attention-to" rather than discovering something hitherto unknown to us.

God's existence is explicitated clearly enough – but not as some kind of reality whom (or which) we encounter at the end of a road, at the close of an argument. God, the UNLIMTED BEING, does not emerge as the superstructure of an intellectual activity. He is discovered as the goal of my very depths, as that which urges me to activity from my very depths. He is active in the very depths of my being. I can now understand the basis of St. Augustine's remark that we are made for God and are so weary until we rest in Him. And St. Ignatius of Loyola's wish that we should find God in all things makes solid, metaphysical sense. Many mystical and theological statement of yore, which might otherwise have sounded like mere dogmatic pious platitudes, are given an in-depth philosophical foundation by Maréchal! Indeed, herein does the whole philosophy of liberation take its roots: God is to be sought in the world – there is no normal shortcut to Him/Her accessible to **pure** effort. Truly, "there is no salvation outside the world"!

The **principle of causality** in its metaphysical or transcendental application is also validated. It is exercised every time we make the metaphysically undeniable activity of direct judgement. Each time we do so, we are asserting the dependence of limited being, ontologically, on the UNLIMTED BEING. In fact, it is this bond that explains why we make direct judgements at all. Remember Maréchal's precise and carefully worded statement of the principle: "whatever is not a being by its very essence depends totally or ontologically on the being that is being by its very essence." Our intellectual dynamism or direct judgement has revealed just that.

The **created nature** of the "things of this world", the realities we affirm in our direct judgement, is also established. For, as we have seen, we are implicitly asserting their total ontological dependence (or participation) on the UNLIMTED BEING. And that is creation seen from the point of view of the creative cause!

The **objectivity of our human knowledge** is also borne out by the analysis of our intellectual dynamism. One of the antinomies of human knowledge is its immanent-transcendent (or its subjective-objective) tension. I read a book and, after it is taken away from me, I can tell you what was in it. That means that somehow what was in the book has passed into me, become me (even while it doesn't leave the book, physically!). Yet, true though it is that the book has, in a very real sense, "become me", yet I know it as not-me, as object (Latin, "*thrown against me*"). How does it come about to know it as not-me? Animals, for instance, also know things, but there is no evidence to show that they know them as objects. As Donceel[2] puts it "they know the things of their environment as **spatially** distinct from themselves but not as **entitatively** distinct." Just as, for example, a dog knows its tail as spatially distinct from itself and I know my little finger as a distinct part of me, in the same way is an animal conscious of a bone or a shoe: it doesn't know it as something not-itself. Now the only way I can know things immanently and yet objectively is if there is such a thing as intellectual dynamism. As Donceel so felicitously puts it:

We know the form of another as the form of another, because we strive towards that form before we have it; when we have it, we continue to desire it, and after having acquired it, we strive past it, beyond it, in our quest for the unlimited being. Of all this our spiritual activity is, at least vaguely, aware.[3]

As Rahner shows us in his penetrating study, *Spirit in the Word*, it is only because our intellect is reaching out towards the infinite that we can think at ll. We know or "grasp" it implicitly as *Vorgriff* (literally *fore-grip*), a term which Donceel renders as self-consciously as "transcending anticipation"!

Other metaphysical truths: there is no need to make a too detailed inventory and a spelling out of every element of these. Suffice is it to mention these in passing. First of all, there is the capacity of the human mind to know truth. Direct judgement is a metaphysical fact and, if we grant (as grant we must) we can attain that truth, then we are forced to admit that we have attained various other implicit truths as well. We have listed some of them. Secondly, the possibility of metaphysics is evident enough for among these principles are to be discerned the very tools and raw material out of which we can fashion our discipline. Finally, the principle of identity (a thing is what it

2 *Natural Theology*, New York, Sheed & Ward, 1962, 89.

3 Ibid, 89-90.

is) and contradiction (a thing cannot be and not be the same thing at the same time and under the same aspect) are also implicit in these. In fact, I could not make an affirmation or a denial of them without implicitly asserting them!

Conclusion

The proof of the pudding is in the eating. I am sure that it is now clearer that the aptness of direct judgement as our choice for a starting point is well established. It has afforded us all we sought for a good deal more besides. This is what the old philosophers would call the *circuminsession of metaphysical verities*, the fact that the fundamental truths and principles of philosophy are so inter-linked (literally, sitting inside of each other) that you can't put your finger on one without touching all of them!

PART TWO

ON BEINGS

Chapter 3

The Analogy of Being

An attempt to establish a working definition of "being": what do we mean when we say "being"? It seems that an analogical understanding of "being" is most apt

a. The Transition

The first two chapters of this treatise served as an introduction to our study. They sought to clarify the *what* and the *how* of metaphysics. In other words, they aimed at giving us a rough general idea of the nature and purpose of metaphysics as also its method. Hopefully we now recognise its relevance and necessity. And if it admittedly seems a bit abstract, hopefully we are able to realise that this is not an abstractness stemming from its being far removed from reality. It is an "in-depth" abstractness, arising from the fact that it provides the very basis and groundwork foundation for all our thinking and acting, including our most down-to-earth activity and action for justice. And metaphysics is more then phenomenology, seeing things as they are and stopping with an interpretation of what we observe. This might end up as little more than an attempt to justify the *status quo*. Metaphysics tries to get to the very heart and core of things – which means getting a glimpse of things **as they should be** in practice, and often are not! Authentic metaphysics can be a very subversive discipline! It challenges the way things actually are, the structures in which we concretely encase persons and things. Whence our transition to part two.

In this second part we have two chapters which busy themselves with beings in general. In a final portion we shall focus on the Being of beings. Now the first question we take up is, naturally enough, "What is being?" And the second, which follows from it, is, "What are the properties, the qualities that belong to any and all beings, from the mere fact that they are beings?" These are the topics for study in this and the following chapter.

b. No mere academic issues

By now the reader should have inferred that were these questions mere "academic issues" we wouldn't have given them much attention. Of course, academic issues have their place in life, especially on a philosophical syllabus. However, we have other priorities. We are Third World people with more pressing agenda and, what is more, we haven't come here to study philosophy for the sake of truth in general. We view philosophy as a means to a pastoral end: our concern is for the Truth that makes people free, our concrete impoverished and marginalised people.

What bearing has the abstract-sounding query, "What is being?" on the lives and struggles of our people? A good deal, to say the least. How I define "being" is going to have a profound influence on my attitude and actions in the world. For instance, if I define being in such a way that only God or the Absolute can verify the definition, then all that makes up this world would be (at least relatively) non-being and would not merit serious attention. On the other hand, were I to define being in such general terms that God, human and sub-human reality would be all equally "being" then it'd be difficult to distinguish God from the rest of reality and we would land up in pantheism. Whatever be our personal liking or not for such a system, we cannot deny that it ends by not taking human responsibility and initiative seriously either (for, in the last analysis, it would be that the Absolute or God is the sole active agent, working through us) and the world situation would not cause us much concern. The murder and mayhem, the injustice and the agony all around us – that would be mere appearances and nothing more. In the ultimate analysis (metaphysically) there would be only the Absolute manifesting itself and acting through a million myriad ways. And we should not take appearance for reality!

Is there a way out of the dilemma of non-realism on the one hand and of pantheism on the other (the terrible options for Sankara and Ramanuja, the great Indian metaphysicians had to face)? My answer is yes – by way of the analogy of being. There is no other way!

c. Terminology

Now, before we set about showing that the analogy of being is the solution to get us out of the impasse we spoke of and then go on to demonstrate that, in actual fact, our activity of direct judgement implicitly uses the notion of being analogously, we need to clarify the various terms relevant to the whole business of language usage. Perhaps nothing in all this will be really new. It may have well be seen in logic and elsewhere. In which case it'd be more a question of assembling what we already know than learning something totally unknown.

Language implies words and concepts and both of these we, in some way or the other, refer to things – the things about which we speak (or write). Concepts may roughly be defined as mental signs of things and words as verbal signs of things. In practice we could, at least for the moment, identify concept with meaning. Granting this, it shouldn't be too difficult for us to recognise that though concepts may remain the same for different people, the actual words used by various languages to refer to a given thing may be quite different. For instance, a thing with four legs that wags its tail and barks, summons up the same concept in different people, no matter what language they may speak. Yet, each of these people still uses a different word to designate that reality (or sum up its concept.) An Englishman will say dog, a Hindi-speaker will say *kutta*, a Frenchman *chien* and a German *Hunde*. All these sounds are chosen arbitrarily, by pure convention. It would be ridiculous to ask which of the above words is more "fitting" or "natural" to apply to the things concerned. Neither spoken word nor its (corresponding) written equivalent in any way imitates the shape of the animal nor the sound it makes! In fact, there is even no correspondence between the sound of the word in question and the way it is written. That too is purely arbitrary. The element of the arbitrariness and conventionality that is part and parcel of every language we note in passing for the moment. Let us pass on to show we actually use words and their corresponding concepts.

Sometimes we come across a case where one word and one single concept or meaning are applied to one unique reality. This is so with all proper names, such as JDV, Pune, India, John Paul II and so on. Such a linguistic usage is called **singularity**. However, if all linguistic practice were to be like this – if we had separate word for each and every individual existent – it would be utterly impossible to communicate! Would be speakers would have to know an infinite number of words several times over!!

Happily, there is the more frequent occurrence of **univocity**. Most of our words are of such nature. Here, a single word, with the same, identical meaning is applied to a host of different realities, all individuals within a particular species. Thus, the word horse or cat or dog is referred to each of the various specimens of the animals in question that inhabit the globe.

At the other end of the spectrum, as it were, we find **equivocity**. In this case, one and the same word is used, with varying meanings or concepts, and is given to things that are totally different from each other. An example is the word **date**. It has at least three different meanings (concepts): (a) A particular fruit (b) A time period indicated on a calendar and (c) An appointment with a loved one of the opposite sex. Or take, as another example, the term **bark**. It could refer either to the sound made by a dog or to the outer covering of a tree. There is no logical reason why, in either case, the same verbal sound should be used with reference to such divergent beings: pure arbitrariness, again. And yet, so it is in every language.

> *Being – id quod suo modo existit – is that which exists in its own way.*

Analogy is a kind of halfway house between the two extremes of univocity and equivocity. An analogous word, then, is one which is applied to many things with a meaning somehow the same and somehow different. Now this "somehow the same and somehow different" can, itself, allow for two further understandings. It could imply, on the one hand, that part of the definition is verified by one of the things concerned while another part of that same definition is not. For instance, we talk about the foot of a human being and the foot of a hill. The word "foot" is used analogously here, in the sense that the foot of the hill partly fulfils the definition of foot, which the human foot does completely – inasmuch as "foot", in both cases, indicates the lowest part of the reality referred to. But a person's foot is not merely the lowest part of his/her body: it is also his/her instrument of locomotion, whereas the "foot" of the hill cannot enable it to displace itself. This is a case of what we might call **extrinsic analogy**. But there is another situation, called **intrinsic analogy**, where all the things concerned verify the definition of the word totally, but to different degrees. Take, for instance, the word "life" which we had defined[1] as "self-perfective activity." Now, we recognise that plants, animals and human beings all have self-perfective activity. The plant has, however, the lowest level of self-perfective activity: nourishment, reproduction, growth and repair. The animal has, besides these "vegetative" activities, also locomotion and sensitivity, which the plant doesn't have. Finally, human person enjoys all of these and, over and above them, is alone capable of conceptual language, religion and creative breakthroughs. Each of these three groups have "life" but, while they fully verify the meaning of life, they do it in evidently varying degrees.

d. Towards a definition of being

"Nothing is more practical than a good theory." So said the "master of paradox", G.K. Chesterton. How true this remark is, will soon be borne out of what follows. A little carelessness, a slight ambiguity or clumsiness in formulating a definition of being will have far-reaching effects on our practical and everyday life!

1 Cf. Desbruslais, Philosophy of Human Person, 1997.

If we were to define being, for instance, in a manner that only God could truly fulfil (as "that which necessarily exists" or "that which requires nothing other than itself to account for its existence"), then we would be obliged to call this world of people and things non-being. Hence would stem those various "world-negating" philosophies, as the views of Sankara and Berkeley are traditionally hailed. On the other hand, if we want to maintain the reality of this world while still accepting the above definition of being, the only way out would be via pantheism: maintaining that this would is but, fundamentally, an expression of God. This is the way of Ramanuja.

And then there was Sartre, who defined being in terms of two water-tight compartments, *être-en-soi,* being-in-itself (unconscious and static) and *être-pour-soi*, being-for-itself (conscious and dynamic). As a result of this arbitrary approach he literally "defined" God out of existence!

The medieval thinker, Scotus, was one of several philosophers who sought to define being in a purely equivocal manner by identifying being with existence: being is that which exists. By that token God and the things and persons of this world are all beings on an equal footing. Then would result the complex matter of trying to get out of pantheism (if that is a problem for one) by introducing various subtle and confusing distinctions and refinements to the whole discussion!

For all these (not to mention a host of other) reasons, it seems best to fall back upon the traditional scholastic definition of being – *id quod suo modo existit*, that which exists in its own way. As we shall now proceed to indicate, this definition is analogous in nature and so, among other things, is able to save both the transcendence of God and the reality of the world.

God and creatures (the beings of this world – and angels, if we grant their existence) both verify the definition fully: they exist necessarily, with an unreceived, uncreated and unlimited existence. All else exists by virtue of a received, created and limited or finite act of existence. God and creatures each have their "own" act of existence, in their "own way" and the difference lies in their way of existence.

So I am a being, the dog is a being and the cow is a being. What about my height and my weight? Are they beings, too? For scholastic philosophy, yes (and this seems a perfectly realistic answer to me). They certainly "exist" – my height and weight are not illusory by any means. They don't, of course, exist by subsisting (that is, they don't exist "by themselves", by a separate act of Existence, but by "inherence" as the classical term has it.) As we shall see, in scholastic idiom, "accidents" (such as my height And weight) "inhere in the substance", that is, they share in the same Act of existence that I possess in and through my **substance**. We shall be recapitulating all these terms presently.

All these are instances of the notion of being used analogically, with **intrinsic** analogy: that is, the full definition is verified in each case, albeit in different degrees. Do we have any instance of the notion of being used with **extrinsic** analogy, namely, in such a way that the full definition is not always implied?

Well, falling back on the scholastic tradition once more, this is the case when we refer the word **being** to what has been called "possibles" and "relative non-beings". A possible, as the name applies, is not an actually existent being, it is but its concept, an idea. Examples would be the pictures that the artist intends to paint or the poem the poet plans to write. Of course, once these people execute their projects, we no longer have possibles, but an actual landscape or sonnet. Relative non-beings are pure negations, as non-cat or non-dog. However, it is usual to classify "evils" among such, for instance, blindness and cancer. An evil, in the Augustinian-Thomistic tradition is not a positive reality: it is a **privation**, a lack of a due perfection in a positive reality. Blindness is lack of sight in a person or any other being that is meant to have vision. Inability to fly is a privation (hence an evil) in a crow, but not so for a human being. Sickness in general as also in its various concrete manifestations (which would include cancer) is not conceived as a positive entity but as merely the lack of health in a positive reality in which it is due, such as a human person or a dog. Of course, few people nowadays would see cancer or leprosy as a mere lack of health, but as the actual presence in an organism of some noxious germ or virus or whatever. However, medical science had not made many strides in the days of Augustine or Aquinas and so that is why they came to their particular conclusions about disease being a "relative non-being."

Whatever it may be, according to scholastic tradition, we may speak of non-dog, disease and deafness as beings. And then we would be using the word *being* according to extrinsic analogy. The full definition is, let us recall that which exists in its own way. But, as we have seen, these things don't really exist: like possibles, relative non-beings are merely isolated essences. Thus, calling them "being" is like speaking of the "foot" of a mountain or calling God a "rock."

Now I'm sure all of us would have little difficulty (if any) about calling possibles and relative non-beings being, by extrinsic analogy. Where we might have our reservation is whether disease is a relative non-being or not (I, for one, most decidedly do not go along with such understanding). However, that is not the point under discussion at the moment. We were in search of a definition of being, one that would steer us clear between the Scylla of non-realism or a-cosmism and the Charybdis of pantheism. And we have found that definition, "that which exists in its own way" fits the bill admirably, being of itself open to analogous application. As for diseases, well, we won't call them relative-non-beings but actual beings (a concrete disorder in an organism caused by the actual presence of some observed or observable harmful entity).

Then these would be beings by intrinsic analogy. Of course their existence would further complicate the whole question of the mystery of evil which we have to face in the *Philosophy of God*.[2] We leave a fuller reflection on that issue for that particular treatise.

e. The activity of direct judgement implies the analogy of being

The aptness and fittingness of the above definition and the whole notion of the analogy of being is further confirmed by the activity of direct judgement. In other words, a little reflection on what we do when we make direct judgements implies that we implicitly affirm that being is that which exists in its own way and we use it analogously!

We have seen that we affirm essence and existence as properties of a being every time we make a direct judgement. Furthermore, we also implicitly assert that the immediate objects of our direct judgement are partially what the unlimited being is fully: in other words, we are saying that they all fulfil the definition of being but in different degrees. The beings around us are recognised – at least implicitly – as instances of limited, finite beings and our intellectual dynamism drives us beyond these to the affirmation of the unlimited, infinite being. This amounts to saying that we are exercising the analogy of being and that definition of being which we agreed upon whenever we make a direct judgement!

f. A short historical note on the notion of analogy

Thomas Aquinas didn't invent (discover?) the idea: Plato and Aristotle spoke of *analogia*. Neoplatonic and Augustinian examplarism gave it a new development and it came to the Angelic Doctor through his compatriot Albert as also through the medieval Muslim thinker Averroes. There is a pioneering work by Hampus Lyttkens on this subject, *The Analogy between God and the World: An investigation of Its Use by Thomas of Aquino*.[3] And, as Etienne Gilson reminds us, Aquinas never devoted a specific treatise to the question: he discussed it within the framework of other matters, in reply to specific objections. Writes Gilson, "his [Aquinas'] texts on the notion of analogy are relatively few, and in each case they are so restrained that we cannot wonder why the notion has taken on such an importance in the eyes of his commentators."[4] Klubertanz, in a later study[5] has uncovered – and listed (unfortunately for most students in the original Latin only) – some 500 references scattered over his various writings, but he himself admits that the comment on their "restrained"

2 Cf. C. Desbruslais, JDV, Pune, 1997.

3 Uppsala, Almqvist and Wiksells, 1952.

4 *The Christian Philosophy of St. Thomas Aquinas*, trsl. L.K. Shook, New York, Random House, 1956, 105.

5 *St. Thomas Aquinas on Analogy*, Chicago, Loyola University Press, 1960.

nature remains true. Granted all this, we must admit that what emerges from Aquinas is a "a remarkably harmonious and consistent use of analogy."[6]

There is no need to rehearse all we have said about analogy, buttressing the discussion this time with appropriate texts from Aquinas' *corpus*. For that I would refer interested parties to Klubertanz's excellent study. Suffice is it, according to me, to append here what Aquinas says about **analogy of proportion** and **of proportionality**. The distinction crops up for the first time in the *De Veritate* (*On Truth*). In the former there is a resemblance between two things (the numbers 4 and 8, say, where one is twice the other), whereas in the latter the resemblance is between the proportion or relation of one pair of things compared to that of another pair of things (thus, 8 is to 4 as 6 is to 3). To take a non-mathematical example, it would be analogy of proportionality where I to speak of "vision" with regard to ocular as well as intellectual perception. The meaning would be that as corporal vision is to the eye, so intellectual apprehension is to the mind.

Later there developed a big argument among commentators on Aquinas as to whether he went on to abandon analogy of proportionality in favour of analogy of proportion, in the whole business of "God-talk" or attributing perfections to God. This point is irrelevant to us here. However, in passing, I might point out that in his famous *Commentary on the Sentences* he was to list both types of analogy and the mere fact that he emphasises proportion more than proportionality in his more mature works as the *Summa* and the *Contra Gentiles* is no conclusive evidence that he had shelved the notion!

In conclusion, let us remark that unless one were to go along with the most drastic of monistic systems, we would be compelled to admit that the things around us are not plainly and simply of a piece and yet, in order to make such a plurality intelligible, some kind of basic unity within the diversity has to be admitted. In other words, some kind of theory of analogy of being is inevitable for practical everyday life and communication.

6 Ibid, 111.

Chapter 4

Transcendentals

What are the necessary qualities or properties of being, those which pertain to all beings from the mere fact of "being a being"? These qualities are called "the transcendentals."

a. The issue

We've just established a kind of common name and definition for all existents, be it God, my mother, a mango tree, a dog or a stone that I'm taking about: they are all "beings" and each of them "exists in its own way". But, quite naturally, we might feel ourselves provoked to ask: is that all? Can we discover any other qualities that necessarily flow from the very essence of beings and that are equally common to all kinds and levels of being? In other words, can we enrich our grasp of being, of reality by bringing out any common properties (qualities that necessarily follow from its very nature or essence) that belong to each and every being? There are, after all, certain properties that pertain to a particular kinds of being: all "aquatic" being has the property of freezing at a particular temperature, all human beings have rationality, all plants take nourishment and so on. In a similar way, are there any properties that pertain to aquatic being, human beings, plant life and so on? This is the question before us in this chapter. In metaphysical language, the technical term for these is **transcendentals**.

b. Why "transcendentals"?

The dictionary tells us "to transcend" means, in general to go beyond. Thus, we may say that a student's prowess in the exams "transcended" his wildest dreams. Just as *as-cend* means to go up *de-scend* means to go down, *trans-cend* means to go beyond, or surpass. Now, the qualities alluded to above are called "transcendentals" because they go beyond the particularities of the various kinds or levels of being and pertain to them all. Immanuel Kant used the word in the same sense when he spoke, in his *Critique of Pure Reason*, about the "transcendental aesthetic" and the "transcendental logic". In those sections of his work, he was exploring respectively the workings of our sense faculties and our rational faculties, "going beyond" the specifications of what is being known in each case: he was trying to sift out what is common to all acts of sense-knowledge, whether it be a cow, a concert or a football match that I am perceiving. So also with intellectual knowledge. In so doing, he was but borrowing a term from the scholastic tradition which he always respected, even if he hardly felt in agreement with it.

Most contemporary scholastic thinkers are content with the term as it stands. Thus, we find the word "transcendental" endorsed by authoritative texts by Emerich Coreth sj, Martin O Vaske sj, Robert Kreyche, Herman Reith and so on. However, another neo-scholastic Leo Sweeney sj, an American, prefers to say "transcendents", because of Kant's use of the older form, "as well as for other reasons"[1]. As Sweeney himself reminds us, Aquinas used *transcendens* (plural *transcendentes*: literally, transcending[s]) rather than *transcendentale* (plural: *transcendentlia*).[2] Be that as it may, I prefer to stick to the older term and I have no particular hassles with Kant's usage of it.

c. Relevance of this quest

At first blush, this may seem to be but another big fuss over "words, words, words" as Hamlet once expostulated. What difference does it make to our ordinary everyday life (especially that of the oppressed) to go on seeking out alleged "transcendentals"? Besides, if these qualities are co-extensive with being, transcending their various classes, then they turn out to be synonyms of being, inasmuch as in the last analysis they would be really identical with being itself. In that case, if being and these properties are identical, why make a distinction between them at all? The answer is that, due to our limited human knowledge, we do not clearly glimpse all the richness of being in "one grand intuition". We need to adjust our point of view slightly so that the various other dimensions of being swim into our ken. Nor are these transcendental

---

1 *A Metaphysics of Authentic Existentialism*, New Jersey, Prentice-Hall, 1965, 154, footnote 43.

2 Cf. *Disputed Questions on Truth*, 21, 3.

properties of being mere vague synonyms – like "thing" or "something" – that do not, in effect, throw any new light on reality. As we shall see, we discover that all being, in proportion to its grade of being, is one, true, good, beautiful and so on. Thus, while these properties are given some of kind of objective status, so also the various human sciences and disciplines that grow out of these respective qualities (mathematics, ethics, aesthetics and so on) are thereby afforded a metaphysical foundation. The relevance of this study, then, should be more than evident!

d. Our method

How will we set about unearthing, as it were, these transcendental properties of being? Obviously we cannot start with an exhaustive phenomenological survey of all beings, endeavouring to sift out the qualities common to the whole spectrum. Besides being obviously tedious and impractical, it is assuredly impossible: how, for instance, would we set about examining God, let alone the countless billions of billions of entities that throng the microcosm and macrocosm? And it would be avowedly dangerous to generalise from a few select instances. There is every likelihood that we be biased in our selection and what guarantee would we have that our favourite findings be validly extended to all of reality – God included! Instead we will train our sights on the direct judgement. We saw that direct judgement is objective, is a metaphysical fact and it is geared to the affirmation of reality. Through it we can reach directly or indirectly all that exists. Our procedure would consist simply in analysing the structure of the direct judgement: we shall find that it implies the affirmation of certain properties of being – that all being is one, true, good and so on. We shall now take up each transcendental in turn and approach the matter in several steps: (a) explain the meaning of the property we are busy with, (b) show how it is implicitly affirmed in the very act of making a direct judgement, (c) draw some practical conclusions from this discovery, applying it to everyday life and to the efforts of the human sciences.

e. The discovery of the transcendentals

A: Transcendental: No. 1: Every being is TRUE
i.e. TRUTH is a transcendental property of being.

Clarifying of terms

Let us note, at the onset, that we are NOT speaking of truth in the following "usual" senses of the term, but rather in its most basic sense, the one on which all these are founded:

Logical truth: correspondence between (contents of the) mind and reality. Thus my idea or knowledge of a dog is true if it corresponds to the reality concerned (here, a dog). This is the understanding of the truth we are busy with in epistemology.

Moral truth: correspondence between what I know and what I say: its opposite would be what we call a "lie". This is the kind of truth we explore in ethics.

Ontological truth in the DERIVED sense: correspondence of some reality to the idea or plan of it. Thus, if a chair is made by a carpenter in such a way that it conforms to the pattern that he had intended, it is "true". To the extent that it fails to do so (either due to the defects of the raw material or the lack of skill in the carpenter) it may be said to be a "false" chair with regard to what was intended by its maker.

Ontological Truth in its MOST BASIC sense: by this is meant the basic intelligibility of a thing – in other words, every being is knowable. Of course, this doesn't mean to say that any being (let alone God) is exhaustively known by us, but that it is accessible to our cognitive faculties.

Demonstration:

In the direct judgement, as we have seen, we affirm immediately and directly the beings of this world as having existence and essence and, mediately and directly, the unlimited being in which they participate and from which they derive their reality. This implicitly affirms also that I have the capacity to know being (subjective dimension) and that being is, consequently, knowable (objective dimension). Thus the basic intelligibility of being is a necessary pre-condition for the direct judgement – which is a metaphysical (i.e. undeniable) fact.

Conclusions

The basic intelligibility of being, as discovered from this analysis, can serve as the metaphysical foundation for our intellectual research into the mysteries of the world around us (and within us!). Inasmuch as we implicitly affirm the knowability of God in every direct judgement, this provides us with a solid basis for our desire to quest for God and even to desire that he freely reveals himself to us. But let us hasten to add that we conceive of human knowledge not as a proud *com*-prehension of reality, but as a humble *ap*-prehenion of it!

Metaphysics, as we have just seen, maintains that every being, in so far as it is being, is true. In Heideggerian terms, we could say that every being, by the mere fact that it is endowed with existence, is a claim to be true. It is this basic understandability which is the claim that reality places before us, that constitutes the essence of truth. What we call logical truth is the humble listening response of the intellect to this claim. In this world only the human person can meaningfully respond to this "word" of being. Were we to say "No!" to this claim of reality, we would be blind people, insensitive to the demand of reality, irresponsible "shepherds of being". This would be insincerity, "logical" untruth. If we remain true to our nature ("ontological" truth in its derived form), we have to say "Yes!" to the revelation or disclosure of being. *Satyagraha,* the responsibility of holding fast to the truth, is the basic ontological responsibility of the human person.

B: Transcendental No. 2: Every being is ONE
i.e. UNITY is a transcendental property of being.

Clarification of terms:

Unity, in general, implies a certain inter-connectedness within and a separation from others. But there are degrees of unity:

Perfect unity: total absence of parts: such unity we find only in God.

Imperfect unity: parts, but somehow linked together: this is the level of unity that we find, in various degrees, among creatures. We may further subdivide this imperfect unity we find in creatures according to the way in which the "linking together" is brought about:

Through intrinsic links: the unity is brought about by a kind of "inbuilt link" in the very inner structure of the being. This is the case in all "natural" being (not made by human beings or other creatures), and especially in living beings. Thus, the inner structure of a human person or a cow holds together the various parts to make it a single unit. So also, though to a lesser degree of integration, a plant.

Through extrinsic links: the unity is brought about by some kind of exterior links that hold the whole together. Such do we find in all "artificial" beings or artefacts (made by humans or animals). Thus a book is held together by gum, thread, etc. A table consists of several distinct pieces of wood joined together by nails, screws and gum. A bird's nest is kept together by interwoven twigs, festend together by mud or whatever.

Demonstration

In the direct judgement we always affirm "This is an X". In other words, we affirm an integration of existence and essence as constituting a particular being and thereby rendering it one and separate from all others. Thus implicitly, every direct judgement asserts the oneness of being.

Conclusions

What we are asserting here is not the absolute unity of all reality (monism), but the internal cohesion that is at the heart of every being, making it what it is. From this we derive the metaphysical principle of identity: "A thing is what it is." It can also be re-stated in its contrary form as the principle of contradiction: "A thing cannot be and not be the same thing at the same time and under the same aspect." A mango can be green at one time and yellow at another time: it can't be both yellow and green at the same time. Or, perhaps, one part of it may be green and another part yellow at the same time. Here, the mango is green and yellow at the same time, but under different aspects.

Oneness, metaphysically speaking, always implies certain internal synthesis (inner cohesion, as we have said above) plus an external separation (it is not part of others). This does not mean that a being cannot be "grouped together" with others on the basis of some common qualities found among them all – like an individual piece of chalk, lying in a box of chalk. Yet, while sharing in a certain commonality with others of the same ilk, it restrains its own individuality. Indeed, it is this individuality plus commonality that makes counting possible – the basis of arithmetic and its allied disciplines.

The basis of the commonality, whereby we perceive some kind of unity bonding together various individuals, is varied. It can be on the grounds of a common genus or species: this is logical unity. Thus we group together all species of dogs as well as all individual dogs under the common heading of canine being. However, there is no reality corresponding to "canine" as such existing in the world in concrete form. Since the basis for this unity is an idea or concept, we call this logical unity, as we saw above. But we can speak of the real unity of the pieces of chalk in the box. The classification "chalk" actually exists in reality and it is this which affords the grounds for perceiving a unity in "chalk" being. When free beings come together to form a group on the basis of some common project or goal – a Church, a nation or a debating society, say – we have what we call a moral unity, since it results from the free choice of morally acting beings. Note that in this paragraph we are speaking of external unity: that is, a group or collection of individuals who come together under some common heading while retaining their particular individuality. This reminds us that we can never countenance a system which demands that the individual be completely swallowed up into the group, losing its own individuality forever.

Finally, the principle of uniformity of nature – which Hume questioned and on which scientific laws (form which stem all our technological advancement) – can also be shown to follow from the transcendental property of oneness, as a corollary of the principle of identity and contradiction. This transcendental, demonstrated by the direct judgement, gives a metaphysical basis to that assumption upon which scientific research and progress are made. When, for instance, a chemist tells us the molecular composition of water or a physicist spells out the laws of motion, the former is maintaining that his finding holds true of all water, wherever it is found, and the physicist says that all motion, whatever it involves, abides by these laws. If there were no constancy in these things, if nature were not uniform in its behaviour, then we could not build upon previous discoveries and inventions and there could be no scientific development. It is the transcendental of oneness that gives a solid metaphysical basis to what we can only otherwise "take for granted". By now it should be becoming more and more evident why we call metaphysics "the first science" the discipline that provides all other disciplines with their basis.

C: Transcendental No 3: Every being is GOOD
i.e. GOODNESS is a transcendental property of being.

Clarification of terms

Though at first sight, goodness seems to be a word whose usage is restricted to the moral sphere and is, more or less, a synonym of holiness or moral perfection in that regard, we must not forget that everyone also uses this word in other contexts. For instance, rather loosely we may speak of a "good" movie, a "good" answer or even a "good" goal! The most basic meaning of "good", underlying all these expressions is "that which brings some perfection", i.e. some positive, desirable quality to another. A "good" movie is one that brings entertainment or food for thought, a "good" answer is one which helps to satisfy one's quest for knowledge, a "good" goal is on which not only secures a point for the side but which also gives evidence of a player's skill! As St. Thomas Aquinas wrote, "the essence of goodness consists in this, that something be perfective of another in the manner of an end."[3] We might also remember[4] that, whereas "the true" is the formal object of the intellect (i.e. It is the aspect under which I mind encounter reality), "the good" is the formal object of the other spiritual faculty, the will. But there again we are using the word in a rather restricted sense. Let us now gather all the senses that are directly or indirectly related to this term.

Goodness in the most GENERAL sense: suitability for an appetite. Again, we normally use "appetite" with reference to our desire for food only (but we do speak occasionally of the "sex appetite" and so on). Appetite, in general, means an inclination or a craving for that which brings about some fulfilment or enrichment in a conscious being (Latin: *ad* + *petitio* = a calling for, an inclination to). Appetite is subjective: it points to something in the being that makes it go out of itself in search of another. Goodness refers to the capacity in this other to fulfil an appetite. Even when something evil or sinful is sought after by a moral being, it is sought after under the aspect of a good that it brings; some sensual pleasure or an escape from pain. The relevant moral question to be asked is whether the procurement of this limited good would lead to one's all round betterment or perfection – would it make one a better person? – or

> *We can discover the truth of the oft-quoted dictum that "holiness is wholeness".*

3 *Disp. Questions on Truth*, XXI, 2.

4 See Desbruslais, *Philosophy of the Human Person*, JDV, Pune, 1997.

would it give merely an isolated, disproportionate and momentary happiness that, in the long run, would **not** contribute to one's overall growth?

Physical goodness: that which fulfils some material need or a sense faculty. Thus fresh air, clean water, healthy food and sanitary housing are physical goods, fulfilling our various bodily needs. Colour is good for the eye, sound is good for the ear. But sound is not "good" for the eye, since the latter has no appetite or inclination (pre-disposition) for it.

Metaphysical goodness: that which fulfils more than mere material needs, or which is suitable for our so-called "spiritual" faculties. Thus God is the highest of all (metaphysical) goods, for God alone can bring total satisfaction or fulfilment to our personal (more than merely physical) needs. Keeping the analogy with appetites (cf. above) we could define, metaphysical, or better, ontological goodness as that which fulfils a spiritual appetite (in this case, the will; after all truth is that which fulfils the other spiritual appetite, the intellect. We could, in this sense, say that Truth is "the good" of the intellect).

Other related senses of "good" include the following (these are mentioned in order to avoid confusion of meanings and misunderstandings):

- *the useful*: good for the same of something else. Thus a cycle is good for the one who wants to go to town.
- *the worthy*: good for its own sake, and not as a means to something else. A person is good or respectable or loveable in this sense.
- *the delightful or enjoyable*: the good that brings aesthetic or sensual pleasure. Thus, we may speak of having had a "good' meal or a "good" game of basketball. But, as we probably have noticed, especially when we speak of "aesthetic good", we are beginning to blur this property with another transcendental, the beautiful. About this ontological quality, more later.

Demonstration

In the direct judgement, as we have seen, we implicitly assert the basic intelligibility (=ontological truth) of all beings. This means that every being carries within it an objective property (intelligibility) which makes it good for the intellect. Now, the will follows the intellect. Hence, as soon as this goodness is presented to it, the will recognises this good as something which it can choose or set aside for another, higher good. Thus every direct judgement implicitly affirms the ontological goodness of being.

Conclusions

The recognition of this transcendental gives us a strong basis for moral philosophy and philosophy of values. It also assures us of the basic goodness of all that we encounter. This liberates us from an pessimistic metaphysics or any manicheanistic attitudes which see certain (material!) beings as intrinsically evil as opposed to other ("spiritual") beings which alone are "good in themselves".

We can also discover the truth of the oft-quoted dictum nowadays that "holiness is wholeness". Perfection or all-round development is to provide for the full flowering of one's nature, the satisfaction of all one's appetites or inclinations. However, we can see that it is up to us to use freedom to ensure the proper harmonisation of our various appetites, who often clash among themselves. For instance, my appetite for food, if indulged in unrestrained might give a measure of fulfilment to my appetite for food … to the extent of making me ill and thus ruining (at least for a time) my personal enrichment. It is my responsibility to so orient my activity that my "physical" appetites (which cater for isolated needs in isolation from my overall well-being) are subordinated to my "spiritual" appetites (which see to the actualisation of my overall personal needs). The authentic "good" person aims at the harmonisation and integration of all his/her needs and appetites in a manner which truly makes him/her the image of God, the all-perfect (in the sense of fully actualised) one.

The metaphysical **principle of finality** may be viewed as a corollary of third transcendental, just as the principle of identity and contradiction derive from the fact that all being is one. This principle says that every being acts for the sake of an end. No action is done without a conscious or unconscious inner orientation towards some goal or purpose (good). Even an "involuntary action" like rubbing one's nose or scratching one's head is done (unconsciously) to remove discomfort or facilitate some activity. Fundamentally, every action of ours – as of all creatures – is ultimately a more or less clumsy, more or less conscious quest to love, and be loved by God. Our intellectual dynamism drives us out of ourselves in search of Being. A little reflection will open our eyes to the realisation that our need to know being soon becomes more focused as a drive to know persons (i.e. there is a dynamism from knowing impersonal being to knowing person). This intellectual dynamism soon develops into a volitional and a totally personal drive to love persons and it is in and through this experience and quest for inter-personal love that we are led to know and love God. This loving encounter transforms us and sends us forth in greater love to our brothers and sisters and to action for the sake of the kingdom – that is, commitment to ensuring the all-round flowering of all beings.!

D: Transcendental: No 4: Every being is BEAUTIFUL
i.e. Beauty as a transcendental property of being

Clarifications

Once again, we have to make an effort to broaden our understanding of this term. We tend to use it in an exclusively physical sense: we call "beautiful" that which delights our sense faculties only. Aquinas himself recognises that the common understanding of beauty (*pulchritudo*) is *quod visum placet* (that which pleases on being seen). However, it should be clear from the context that he is taking "being seen" in a wider, more metaphorical sense. For we can have a beautiful sound (strictly inaccessible to the eye) and there is also a beauty of personhood and virtue which can hardly be known by the sense faculties alone! Hence, we have:

Beauty in the most general sense: that which pleases a cognitive (i.e. a knowing) faculty. This sub-divides into two inasmuch as we have two levels of cognitive faculties:

Beauty in the physical sense: that which pleases one or more sense faculties; thus, we may speak of the beauty of a well-proportioned body, of a choir singing in harmony and so on.

Beauty in the metaphysical sense: that which pleases a spiritual faculty: that is, a faculty which can go beyond the merely physical. We, in this context, might speak of a beautiful friendship or a beautiful thought.

But just how do we distinguish the **good** from the **beautiful**? They are inherently related, the beautiful being a form of the good. However, whereas goodness pertains to what is accessible to the tendential faculties (e.g. the will), the beautiful comes under the purview of the cognitive faculties (the senses and the intellect).

What is it that pleases one in a beautiful object? The clarifications given above only tell us **what** a beautiful thing does to us: it pleases those who know it. But **how** does it please us? What constitutes this beauty? Of course, there are many definitions. There is the well worn scholastic formula: the splendour or order. First, beauty implies a certain order, proportion or harmony. I would like to take one step further and say that the essence of this "order" is basically "unity in diversity". Utter uniformity is boring, discordant differences are ugly. Of course, people of varied cultural backgrounds may disagree as to whether a particular assemblage of qualities is harmonious (order) or not. Three would be no differences about what they see: the various proportions and blends of colour and proportion. But there could very well be vast areas of opinion as to whether that constituted order and harmony! We cannot deny that there is a certain subjective element in the perception of aesthetic (or physical) beauty! The word "splendour" implies that this order should strike or overwhelm us: it should shine out from the being (Latin s*plendor* = a shining forth).

Demonstration

In the direct judgement we affirm that being is suitable for the intellect (inasmuch as it is knowable or ontologically true) and also of or the will (inasmuch as it is perceived by the will as good). In other words, it has a quality that gives pleasure to the subject through his spiritual and cognitive faculties. This means that it is ontologically beautiful.

Conclusions

Note that we are talking about ontological beauty: the ability of being to delight our cognitive faculty. Thus a particular being may be physically or aesthetically ugly (it does **not** delight our sense), for instance, some people find frogs or lizards ugly. When we say that a being is ontologically beautiful, we mean that it is capable of giving delight to our faculties of knowledge (at least our intellect): we want to know: knowledge gives us delight and that quality inherent in the things that we know, whereby they afford us delight through our knowledge of them constitutes their ontological goodness.

This transcendental property of being, viewed with precedent, assures us that not only is no being inherently evil, no being is inherently ugly! This, among other things, should motivate us to work for justice and the full flowering of God's kingdom. For, if we come across anything or any state of being appears to us as evil and ugly, we realise that it is not meant to be so by its very nature but that it has been "twisted out of shape" as it were. To work for justice is to fight against what has rendered a being ugly and evil and to restore it to its original state of goodness and beauty. The Book of Genesis shows us God viewing each of the things he had made, in turn, and affirming each time its goodness ("And God saw that it was good.") We could just as well have been presented with God affirming the essential beauty of all that he made. ("And God saw that it was beautiful!") All this gives a worthwhile foundation to our study of aesthetics and of art.

What is beauty, after all, but the integrated intuition of the oneness, goodness and truth of that is, of each being? And can we not see in these triple-transcendentals a kind of mirror of the trinity? For the Father is the One without second. The Son is the Truth become flesh in the Word of God. Finally the Spirit is the gracious goodness of God overflowing into our lies. Can we not find in these transcendental attributes of every single being – one being with three basic properties that cannot be merely identified with each other while not impairing the essential unity of the being in question – a better analogy to discover the significance of the Trinity in our lives than the traditional three-persons-one-substance formula? We shall see, later, how this also links up with the traditional Indian recognition of *sat-cit-ananda* as the characteristic of *atman* in its deepest depths!

We turn now to another, final two transcendentals, also inextricably linked. They have not so ancient a history as their predecessors. But they have been at least implicitly recognised as being bound up with the former. Whatever it be, I think they need special underscoring as they point to two very important and relevant properties of being in the contemporary context.

E: Transcendental No 5: Every being is active
i.e. Activity or dynamism as a transcendental

Clarification

Activity is one of those "primary notions": a basic term that we all immediately understand, one that cannot be broken down into anything simpler in order to explain it. However, when we hear the word "activity" or "dynamic", that invariably conjures up images of running, jumping and the like. Indeed, were anyone to ask us to mention what we would consider the most active or dynamic of all verbs, there is every likelihood that we would come up with one of the two listed above. We would hardly think of "to be" as an activity. It sounds like a mere inert fact, rather than a dynamic act. Yet, a little reflection should make us realise that, in point of fact, it is the most active and dynamic of all verbs. Furthermore, all other activities are nothing but a spilling over of the level of "to be" that a particular being possesses. As we shall see later (in part three of this book), life is but a particular intensity of "to be"!

Demonstration

In the direct judgement we affirm of every being that it is (besides that it has a certain nature). In other words, direct judgement recognises "to be" or existence as an undeniable constituent of every being we affirm. Hence, all being is active or dynamic, with the basic underlying activity or dynamism of "to be".

Conclusion

This transcendental provides us, along with the next one, with a firm basis for a dynamic view of reality. As we shall be going into a deeper reflection on the act of being in Part Three, we won't go into it here.

F: Transcendental No 6: Every being has Duration

i.e. Duration as a transcendental

Clarifications

Duration in general: unity of activity. There are different levels of duration, depending on the level of activity of the being concerned. These may be subdivided as follows:

Eternity: the unity of simplicity of the most perfect activity. This is "the duration of God". His activity is undoubtedly the most perfect, there is no discrepancy between what is intended and what is actually realised (as there is in the best of human artefacts), the activity is a generous outgoing and is not due to any inner lack, and so on. And there are no parts in God (for parts are characteristics of materiality), the unity in him (whether it concerns his activity or anything else) is always a unity of simplicity, not of composition (as in material being). Boethius, quoted by Aquinas, defined eternity as "simultaneous whole and perfect possession of interminable life"[5] The "simultaneous-whole" implies an existence which is all at once and not given part after part or act after act in succession (as is the case with creatures). For instance, I do not exist "all at once": my existence is spread out over a series of years, days, hours, minutes, and seconds, following in succession. The "perfect possession of interminable life" refers to the absolute fullness of being, held firmly and in the peace of permanence ("interminable", that is, having no terminus) and immutability (unchangingness). Unlike the "now" of time, it is not fleeting or incomplete. As for the mention of "life", this is to recall that though God is not in a state of becoming, it does not mean that She/He is static and inert: "life" implies Perfect Being which is Perfect Activity. Eternity implies existence without successive duration. As Aquinas puts it, "eternity is the measure of a permanent being, while time is the measure of movement (change)".[6]

Time:[7] the unity of succession of corporal activity. This is the duration of material, mutable (changing) beings. The activity concerned here is corporal (embodied) activity, such as locomotion, growth, nourishment, repair, reproduction and so on. In such activities there is always a succession, one phase follows after another: first I am a baby, then I am child, after that I attain the stages of adolescence and adulthood and so on. This succession is most clearly comprehensible in the case of bodily movement from one place to another. This reminds us of Aristotle's definition of time: "The measure of movement according to before and after."[8] The actual measuring of time may be done either with reference to changes within the material being that is considered or with reference to some other embodied thing. Thus, we can speak of two kinds of time:

Internal time: when the movement or change is measured with reference to some internal states or changes in the being. Thus, if I say, "during my childhood", or "while I was in bed with fever" we have examples of internal time.

External time: here the movement or change is measured with reference to some material being other than the one considered. The most common form of time in this regard is solar time, where we measure the movement according to the revolution of the earth round the sun: thus we have units such as days, years and so on. There is also *sidereal* time, where we measure movement with reference to the orbits of the stars. Examples of this kind of time we find in astrology columns and horoscopes: "When Mars was in the ascendant" and

5 ST, Ia, 10, 1, obj. 1.

6 ST, Ia, 10, 4c.

7 A more elaborate discussion on time from a scientific and philosophical perspective could be found in Kuruvilla Pandikattu, *It's Time!*, JDV, Pune, 1997.

8 *Physics*, Book Delta 11.

so on. There are various other forms of external time. For instance I may say, "There was silence for the space of an Ave" or "In the time you can say 'Jack Robinson' he was back!"

Demonstration

In the direct judgement we implicitly affirm a basic unity as underlying the make-up of every being as also the fact that activity is equally a transcendental property of being. Since duration is nothing but unity of activity, it follows that all being has duration, a duration that is proper to its level of being and of activity.

Conclusions

It is to the great philosopher, Henri Bergson, that we owe the focus on duration as a transcendental property of being. The usual scholastic list stops at one-true-good-beautiful. It is thanks to this eminent thinker of the Philosophy of Life Movement that we have a valuable metaphysical foundation for that dynamic world view that is characteristic of our contemporary age.

Form this fact we can draw many important – pastorally relevant – conclusions. For instance, since ours is not a world of static, finished essences but is ever "in the making", we should not close ourselves to the possibility of development, change and progress. Of course, we should not be so naïve as to assume that progress is inevitable: we should critically monitor the changes that we consciously or unconsciously bring about or endorse, asking ourselves whether these would promote the well-being of the entire cosmos, the humanisation of the community or, as Gandhiji put it with special reference to our Third Word condition: "Will this change be of help to the poorest of the poor in my land?"

Rather than childishly oppose all manner of structures as inhibiting (without structures there can be no community nor any communication), we should advocate dynamic structures, structures that not only allow for variations in different places but also all for continual revision, development and evolution.

Finally, this transcendental provides the foundation for those human sciences like history and sociology which study human activity over a space of time.

Note 1: Analogy and Homology

We have already seen what analogy is. Just as the notion of being is analogous (is applied to all beings in a manner which is partly the same and partly different: the meaning is the same in all but it is realised in different degrees), so also the transcendentals, which are "convertible" with being (can be exchanged with it or substituted for it) are also referred to being in an analogous way. Thus, for instance, unity, truth and goodness are found in God infinitely and in finite being in a finite way.

But within each being taken separately, all the transcendentals are found in a manner proportionate to the level of that being. In other words there is a certain equality of all the transcendentals within the being. In other words there is a *homology* (equal ration, proportion or harmony: Greek *homos* = the same).

Analogy brings out the variety there is in the whole spectrum of beings. Homology reveals the harmony there is within each being.

Note 2: The Principle of Sufficient Reason

Put briefly, this principle states, "Whatever exists has a sufficient reason for its existence, either in itself or in another." This may be valid enough as principle go and some people would like to speak of it as a corollary of the transcendental property of being: truth. The intelligibility of a being, they would argue, lies either in itself or in another. Indeed, rationalists like Leibniz went out of their way to publicise and popularise this formula. It is evidently our old friend, that Principle of Causality, decked out in more rationalistic dress. However, since Hume‘s objections quite effectively shot down some of our naïve flights of fancy about the "self-evidence" of this principle and since this formulation cannot be demonstrated so easily, I have left aside consideration of this: after all Maréchal‘s transcendental analysis of the direct judgement implies it!

Chapter 5

Change

This serves as a useful context to familiarise ourselves with the Thomistic terminology concerning the metaphysical composition of material beings; critical response

a. The phenomenon

> *What is matter? Never mind!*
> *What is mind? It doesn't matter! (popular jibe)*

When we look around us, one undeniable phenomenon hits us in the face: change. Everything seems to be in a flux: nothing lasts. Even the "eternal hills" get eroded, solid iron rusts and – of course – human beings die. We recall the celebrated dictum of Heraclitus, the pre-Socratic: "Everything changes: nothing remains (permanent)." As the words of the well-known nineteenth century hymn, "Abide with me" puts it:

Change and decay in all around I see.

Indeed, it was the intuition of the essential contingency of all things (things merely are: they don't have to be – in fact they are more in a process of constant transition rather than being in the proper sense) that drove Jean-Paul Sartre to his existential despair. Still nearer to our times, Alvin Toffler, in his classic, *Future Shock*, tells us of the tremendous stress and insecurity that modern people have to live with, inasmuch as they find themselves caught up in such a rapidly changing environment that before they can get themselves adjusted to their particular set-up, it changes. The future arrives before one has had time to get used to the present. This leads to all manner of physical and psychic disturbances. Ascetic-minded people, like Plato and the Buddha counsel us to seek peace of mind and body by extinguishing in us all desire for the perishing things of this world and fix our gaze steadfastly on that which is imperishable. "Our hearts were made for you, O Lord, and, oh, how weary we are till we rest in you!" cries St. Augustine. In point of fact, the very next words of the hymn we have quoted above are:

O, thou who changest not, abide with me!

b. An illusion?

But is change real? When Indian thinkers speak of the world as *maya*, this is not necessarily an avowal of nihilism and a-cosmism (denial that the world exists). More often than not it is a way of asserting the relative unreality of the beings of our daily sense experience – another manner of indicating their contingency. Only the Absolute can be called unqualifiedly real: it exists necessarily, it cannot not-be and depends on nothing else for its existence.

However, some thinkers deny the reality of change altogether. They do not say that we do not observe changes taking place around us. There is no quarrel over the phenomenon. What they do is to reject the validity of sense experience. They prefer to go by reason. Their argument is that reason alone is a valid means of obtaining knowledge; sense experience is defective. Now reason, they argue, reveals that change is impossible. Therefore, following the reliable guide of pure reason and eschewing the false leads of sense experience, we should deny the reality of the phenomenon of change. It is all pure illusion. Let's take a closer look the how they present their case.

c. Parmenides' problem

As we saw in our study of Ancient Greek Thought,[1] the first recorded philosophical exercise in the West came to grief with two rival stalwarts and two antagonistic schools in flat contradiction with each other. Heraclitus and his fellow Ionians, relying more on the information of sense, maintained the reality of change and the illusory nature of permanence. Parmenides and the Eleatic school held directly the opposite view. We leave aside the sophistries of Zeno and take seriously only the poser of Parmenides, which alone is worthy of serious attention.

> *I am the only person in the world I should like to know thoroughly.*[2]

According to Parmenides, all that we can say is "Being is." Reality is a single, uniform and unchanging being (not a becoming). After all, to really change means to acquire something new, something that wasn't there before. Now this

1 Cf. C. Desbruslais, *History of Western Philosophy*, JDV, Pune, 1984.

2 Oscar Wilde, *Lady Windermere's Fan.*

> *Change is "the fulfilment of what exists potentially, in so far as it exists potentially."*

"something new" which is allegedly acquired in a change must be either a being or a non-being: there is no "third possibility". But being cannot change by acquiring being, for that is nothing new: it is already being. Nor can it change by acquiring non-being, since non-being is nothing: acquiring nothing means not changing. Thus, as far as Parmenides and his ilk are concerned, change is shown to be effectively impossible. It is an illusion and no more.

d. Aristotle's answer

It was not until Aristotle, that a clever and pertinent response to Parmenides's dilemma was provided, thanks to his theory of act and potency, which gives a good basis for a dynamic world-view.

To grasp this valuable insight, let us begin with the common parlance term **actual** and **potential**, which (like many of our everyday expressions) come from the Stagyrite's repertoire. Let us take a stone and a mango seed. Both are obviously not a mango tree, but there is a difference. True, neither of them is an **actual** mango tree, but the mango seed is at least a **potential** mango seed: it has a certain orientation, an in-built capacity to become a mango tree, given a certain environment. But the stone is not a potential mango tree at all. There is nothing you can do to it, no environment you can provide it with, which will enable it to evolve into a mango tree someday. Thus, there is a halfway house between being and non-being: potential being. A mango seed is an actual mango seed but a potential mango tree. A stone is an actual stone and not a potential mango tree (it may be potential something else – a statue, say).

Now we can define act and potency. In its most general sense, act means a perfection and potency means a capacity or readiness for a perfection. Potency, in turn may be of two kinds, passive and active. A passive potency is the capacity to receive a certain perfection: for example a man has the capacity to acquire fatness ... An active potency is the capacity to do particular perfective action. The faculty of sight, for instance, has the active potency to perceive colour – but not sound. A human being has the passive potency to acquire philosophical knowledge. But this is only because there is in him/her some active inner disposition for it which a chair say, has not!

To go back to Parmenides: change can be shown to be possible, rationally by introducing Aristotle's definition. The beings of our experience are both actually what they are (a stone or a mango seed) and potentially something else (a statue or a mango tree). When they acquire this "something extra" which they were not potentially, they acquire something genuinely new and so change!

e. Change is not substitution

All change implies some degree of composition. Not only must something new be acquired, but something of "the old" must be carried over to underlie the process. There is something in the stone which remains in the statue, it is the same seed which has now "become" a tree: in other words, something within the seed, some common substratum has survived into the tree. If every single element of the "old being" were totally wiped out and the "new being" was absolutely radically new, then there would be no real change but the annihilation of one being and its replacement or substitution, somehow or the other, by the new one! Now we can understand Aristotle's definition of change: "The fulfilment of what exists potentially, in so far as it exists potentially."[3] By "fulfilment", here, is meant the process of actualising what was existing potentially. The final "in so far as it exists potentially" is added because otherwise we'd be referring to the completed changed, whereas, as we have seen, by change we mean the process of passing from potency to act.

f. Thomistic metaphysics

It is at this stage that we would do well to introduce the basic Thomistic concepts concerning the metaphysical composition of finite being, of finite material being in particular. Later on, we will have occasion to make our critical comments on these well worn terms, many of which have passed into everyone's daily speech – often changing their original meaning and causing no end of confusion in the process!

Felix qui potuit rerum cognoscere causas.
(Happy is he who can know the causes of things!)[4]

Existence and **Essence**: This is the first and most basic composition that we observe in the beings of our experience. As we have seen, when we make the direct judgement (which, let us remind ourselves, is an undeniable metaphysical fact) we necessarily affirm, through it, that a being exists and what it is – these are the elements of existence and essence, respectively. By existence is meant the fact – or more accurately, as we shall see later, the **act** – of its be-ing. By essence we mean all that contributes to what it is. If I say, "There is a horse", I am saying that the being concerned exists and is a horse. Its "horseness" (its basic equine nature, its particular colour, height and so on) is its essence.

Substance and **Accidents**: The essence or "whatness" (Latin, *quidditas*) of a thing comprises two dimensions: that which gives primary or basic determination (=substance) and that which provides further or secondary determination (=accidents). Substance designates what a thing is basically.

3 *Physics*, III.

4 Virgil, *Georgies*.

Accidents tell us what concrete qualities this particular instance of that substance carries along with it. Thus a being is basically a horse or a cat or a human being and secondarily a black horse, a fat cat or a tall human being. Here, horse, cat and human being are substances, while black, fat and tall are accidents. Since the substance is more basic and "stands under" all else that contributes to the whatness of a being, it is so called (Latin, *sub* + *stare* = to stand under). The word "accident" comes from the Latin *ac* + *cidere*, "to add onto". Since this term has a totally different meaning in popular parlance, it might be better to translate the Latin *acccidens* (plural *accidentes*) as **additive**.

At this stage we can, perhaps, best explain the two main types of change: accidental change and substantial change. In an accidental change it is merely the shape or some external qualities of a thing which are changed and not its basic "whatnes". Thus, if I take an undressed log of wood, cut it up into planks and finally make a well-carved, varnished table of it, I have only brought about an accidental change to the wood: its shape and colour (its accidents) have changed, but it has remained wood (which is its substance). However, if I pass an electric current though a mixture of oxygen and hydrogen, I get a totally new substance (water), with a whole new set of properties (=accidents), which cannot be reduced to a mere average of those of its constituents. This is a substantial change. Incidentally, since we have said that in a change something of the old being persists, we might well ask what it is that survives from the starting point of an accidental and a substantial change to carry over into the new being. For an accidental change it is clear: it is the same substance that remains (wood, in the example above), while the accidents have changed. But what of a "substantial" change? If the whole substance has changed what is there from the original that has remained? Scientifically speaking, we could say that the old atoms and molecules of hydrogen and atom have survived in the new product, in a radically rearranged form – but it is they who have survived into the new substance. Metaphysically speaking, we would say that the basic materiality of the original substance (its "prime matter", to use the term that is pertinent here and which we will be explaining soon) is what remains unchanged throughout the entire process.

A final word about what the substance "does". We have already mentioned that it provides primary determination (makes a being most basically what it is). Furthermore, it "possesses" the act of existence. This does not mean that it is to be identified with existence or even that existence is part of the substance as such. This, as we have seen, is because existence and essence are two different levels of reality. Existence in no way determines what a thing is and so cannot be made part of the essence, which does precisely that. Thomists, however, hold that the act of existence resides in the substance as its own proper possession and the accidents exist by borrowing or sharing in the act of existence of the substance. Thus it is said that the accidents inhere in the substance (literally stick on to) which emanates or supports them.

And a last point about the accidents. They are sub-divided into necessary accidents and contingent accidents. We note, in passing, that a "necessary accident" is a contradiction between terms, if we understand accident in the popular sense (i.e. something unintentional, inadvertent, something that happened by chance and not by necessity); this difficulty is cleared away if we substitute "additive" (something added on) for a "accident". A necessary accident/additive is a secondary determination that a particular being may or may not have, but doesn't need to have by its very nature. Thus the ability to speak Chinese or play the piano are contingent accidents/additives for a human person: one is not in any way less a human person because she/she does not have these accidents.

Matter and **Form**: in a material being, the substance is further sub-divided into matter and form, prime matter and substantial form to give their full names. All that we have said above, about substance applies to the substantial form of a material, embodied being. If the substantial form is the principle of *determination* (along with the accidents), making a being what it is, providing its nature and qualities, prime matter is the principle of *indetermination*. It doesn't directly contribute to what a thing is, it merely receives the relevant form. It is what, in effect, makes a being embodied, have "parts outside of parts' to use the traditional definition. It also, being the principle of indetermination, is responsible for the full realisation of the form in a particular being: hence, there is always a multiplicity of "individuals within a species" whenever there is a material being. There is an infinite number (if we may be excused from using such a questionable phrase) of human beings, horses, cats, plants, stones and so on. If we grant the existence of angels, who are "pure spirits", that is, have no materiality (no "prime matter") then we would have to grant that each angel is "a species in itself", a totally new spiritual world, with no other one resembling it – more different than the conventional chalk and cheese!

When we speak of "prime matter", we must be careful not to identify it with material substances, like iron, wood and glass, out of which knives, tables and tumblers may be made. These would be "secondary matter". Prime matter is the source of particularity, the root cause of individuation. In itself, it is not a thing, it has no qualities at all, is not quantifiable: it is pure potency. It has no perfection (or "acts"). It denotes the mere passive capacity to receive a form. As the Scholastics say, it is real but only exists in composition with form, not all by itself. In that case, it would be more accurate to say that prime *matter co-exists* (with form in a concrete being), rather than it exists (this would give the wrong impression that it could be found somewhere in itself, in its natural state).

Conclusions

The problem of the **reality of change** is well accounted for using Aristotle's theory of act and potency. We are able to argue, against Parmenides, as we have seen, that change is real. However, we have also established that something remains permanent, underlying the change, throughout the process. Hence there is an element of permanence, too. Heraclitus seems to have glimpsed this when he spoke of fire as being the archã, or primitive stuff out of which the cosmos is made. He was probably speaking symbolically and not asserting that everything around us is literally composed of fire! It is more than likely that he was implying that there is a basic substratum of permanence underlying the constant flux that surround us: fire is ever changing its form, yet it remains fire!

The problem of the **One and the Many** is resolved, too. The problem refers to the fact that if being is one and it suffices, why is there many? In other words, is the apparent multiplicity of beings around is real or only apparent? Are they really different individuals or actually various parts or manifestations of one single being? If there is only one being, how do we account for the apparent multiplicity or pluralism? If a sheer multiplicity of beings, how do we explain the apparent unity and inter-connectedness that there is in reality? And, let us admit at the outset, it is much more logical to assume that there is one being, rather than many (cf. Parmenides!). After all, if "to be" or existence is the characteristic note of being, then what would there be to provide the multiplicity and individuation of beings?

Once again, Aristotle's approach provides us with an answer. Being is not jut pure existence (as in God's case). In that situation, being would be necessarily infinite, unique and not multipliable. But, as the direct judgement has revealed to us, being is more than just existence, pure and simple. There is also the limiting element of essence in the beings we affirm. Thus there can be several existences limited by several essences. The infinite (unlimited) being is one, unique, and unrepeatable; finite (limited) beings are multiple because of their limiting essences. If there are different essences, we have different types of being. If there is further an element of prime matter within the essence, we have further individuation within the species (many horses, many human beings, many mango trees and so on).

A truly comprehensive metaphysics will provide a basis for both the essential plurality of beings as also their basic inter-connectedness. In practice, however, Western thought has tended to exaggerate the isolatedness of individual beings and has ignored the organic unity that interlinks the cosmos. The Indian world vision, on the other hand, emphasises a holistic understanding of reality, seeing the entire cosmos as a piece, to the point of either ending up in monism or pantheism or being misunderstood as so. Contemporary thinkers are now coming round to recognise the solidarity that there is between all that is. Not only are "the things of this world" intimately linked to the Unlimited Being by participation, there is also a kind of bonding between themselves. It might be a poetic exaggeration to say that every time I move my little finger I rock the farthest star[5] but every exaggeration underscores a sold vein of truth! This essential inter-relatedness of all that is provides us, indeed, with the theme of our next study-topic: relations!

The major area of difference which I share with many contemporary thinkers as regards the Aristotelian-Thomistic metaphysics concerns the conception of matter and spirit. Matter and spirit are seen as diametrically opposed: the one has parts outside of parts and the other has no parts outside of parts. Therefore, matter, on principle, can't make a total reflection, cannot turn back on itself, whereas spirit, having no parts, can. Thus I can know that I know or will to will, but I can't see my seeing anymore than I can tough my left thumb with my left thumb. It is concluded that matter and sprit are "essentially different" and, if a being (like human person) can perform a total reflection (can be present to itself by knowing and willing) whereas a dog or a plant cannot, it is because the former has within itself something that the latter two do not (viz. a spiritual soul).

However, as thinkers like Teilhard de Chardin sj and others argue, all this follows if we assume that matter can in no way ever transcend itself. But what if, as Teilhard suggests, consciousness (presence to self) is a function of complexity? At a minimal level of complexity (such as in the inner structure of a stone or even a plant) there is no consciousness. Still, a plant is capable of more complex reactions to a stimulus than is a piece of iron or a rock. Animals have a higher degree of internal complexity and so consciousness emerges in them. In humans, this complexity is of such a high level of order that total reflection is possible. In other words, once a certain level of complexification is attained in a being, consciousness emerges. Hence a human being can be present to self while a piece of chalk cannot, not because in the human there is something that is missing in the chalk (a spiritual soul, as the scholastics would say), but because there is a greater level of complexity in the former than in the latter. In short, humans can't say to the sub-human world a proud, "I have something you haven't got!" – unless that means that I have in me a greater complexity. But there are no special ingredients in me that are lacking in them!

Let us carefully note that both theories about the nature of matter are based on assumptions and interpretations and not on proofs. Both views equally explain the phenomena concerned with adequacy and sufficiency.

5 In the recent chaos theory, they talk of the "butterfly effect" which implies that the fluttering of the wings of a butterfly in Japan will affect the weather in America! The theory of chaos, they maintain, determines such events and leads to an order in chaos.

There is no way to decide which one I should adhere to, apart from asking myself which way of looking at things fits in best ("clicks with") my implicit value system. The traditional scholastic approach gives me access to an easy rational argument in favour of life after death[6] and also underscores the uniqueness and supremacy of the human person over all other material beings. The latter stresses our oneness with all other beings of our experience (we are all moulded out of the same elements). It can afford us a still more integrated and unified view of the human person. But it makes it a little more difficult, though not quite impossible, to find a reasonable basis for a conviction abut life beyond the grave. In effect, we have to opt for that explanation that bears out best values and our pre-understanding.

6 Cf. C. Desbruslais, *Philosophy of the Human Person*, JDV, Pune, 1997.

Chapter 6

Relations

Even though relations are "the weakest kind of being" and few contemporary theologians would wish to use this notion as a means to enter into the mystery of Trinity, it is worth our while to go into the matter, as we shall see.

a. The question

We have come out – with good reason – in favour of plurality, the real multiplicity of individual beings in the cosmos. Thus we avoid the difficulties which a monistic/pantheistic vision of reality plunges us into: an attenuation of human freedom and the imputation of sin and evil to God. But "an error is an exaggerated truth". If we cannot go along with the implications of monism, we should not ignore the undeniable dimension of reality that it reminds us of, perhaps a bit unbalancedly – maybe. Western thought has overlooked another phenomenon in its eagerness to save the reality of individual beings. It is the mystical, poetical and religious intuition of the harmony and inter-relatedness within reality. No man is an island and no being either. The whole of reality, if not numerically one, is somehow bonded together, inter-linked and related such that to touch, displace or affect one being will cause a chain reaction of effects throughout the cosmos (though perhaps, only the more immediate impact will be noticed by us). This, inevitably, leads us into a reflection on the metaphysical nature of relations. If these are mere figments of our imagination and do not point to something real that binds us together, then the cosmos is naught but a heap of isolated and lonely beings, juxtaposed. But can we affirm the reality of relations without landing ourselves back into the very pitfall we have tried to avoid, monism/pantheism, which Hume, referring to Spinoza's philosophy, once qualified as a "hideous hypothesis"?

b. The phenomenon

We experience relations in our everyday life and a little attention will also enable us to pick out the elements involved in their makeup. For instance, in the direct judgement, the act of knowledge makes a relation between me, the knower and the object, the thing known. Within the object, there is a relation between existence and essence, substance and accidents. Again, I am related to my parents as their child and it is the act of generation that is the basis of it.

Analysing this information which we have noted, we recognise that a relation involves three elements, two beings which are related – one of which is the starting-point and the other the end term of the relationship and, finally, some basis or foundation for the relationship. I also notice that some relationships imply a change in both terms of the link as a result. For instance, my father and I are related by fatherhood and the basis of this relationship – the "act of generating", let us call it – brings about a real change in both parties: a young man becomes a father and I come into existence. Sometimes the relation involves a real change in only one of the two terms. Thus knowledge involves real change in me, the knower: I pass from a state of ignorance to a state of knowledge. On the other hand the object of my knowledge does not undergo any real change from the state of being not known by me to the state of being known by me! Again sometimes the terms of a relation are complete, subsisting beings – as me and my father, the knower and the thing known. But sometimes the relationship is not between complete being, each existing in itself – as in the relationship between existence and essence or substance and accidents. Let us now carry all this data over for critical reflection.

c. Critical reflection

Let us first try to separate out a general definition of relation from the various instances we have detailed above. It is obvious that relation is the weakest of all beings: it merely indicates an orientation, a being toward (*esse ad*), a kind of extrinsic unity between two distinct things.

We may further sub-divide relations into two kinds. The first is the **real relation**, when two real and distinct complete beings are somehow or the other linked or oriented towards each other. Then there is the **logical relation**: here, for instance, we do not have two distinct and separate beings which are referred to each other by the external link of relation. Instead we have one single being which we divide into two parts mentally and then link, by a relationship, that which is already internally joined together! Thus we make a distinction within a table of the existence and essence elements and then link them together as related to each other. In short, a *real relation* exists in reality (e.g. Fatherhood, sonship) whereas *logical relations* exist only in the mind.

We can also speak of the **subject** of the relation, i.e. Its starting point and its **term**. i.e. The being to which the subject is referred to in a relation. Thus, in fatherhood, the father is the subject and the son is the term. In the relation of sonship, it is the other way around. By a correlation, we mean the reference of the term back to the subject. Thus, sonship is the correlation of fatherhood.

Every relation, furthermore, must have some **foundation**, a proximate source from which the relation flows or springs. Thus in fatherhood (and its correlation, sonship), the foundation is the act of generation. When I know a chair, the foundation of this relation is my act of knowledge. Foundations, it will be noticed can be grouped either as mediate or immediate or, again, as dynamic or static. An **immediate foundation** is one which is intrinsic to the subject of the relation, whereas a **mediate foundation** is on which is extrinsic to the subject of the relation. Thus, in the case of the relation of me, the knower, and the book, the thing known, the foundation for this relationship is the act of knowledge. Now the act of knowledge is something real and intrinsic to me. Hence, in knowledge there is an immediate foundation in the subject. But take the correlate of "being known", from the side of the table. This 'being known" constitutes the foundation of the relationship of the book back to me. Now, whereas "the act of knowing" is a real new quality within me, "being known" does not imply any special new quality or perfection that has come to a book, as a result of my knowing it: it remains totally unchanged. Hence the foundation is mediate in the case of the object known, here the book. Or, as I have said, we can re-divide the types of foundations in another way. Thus we have **static foundations** wherein the basis or source of the relationship is some perfection already acquired by the two related beings, or **dynamic foundations** in which the basis of the relation is some action done or received. Static foundations are constituted by some substance, quality or quantity, which is found in the two beings, which are related by similarity or dissimilarity as result. Thus I relate two walls to each other either because they have a similar colour or height or because they have dissimilar colours or heights. On the other hand, I relate together Peter and Paul on the basis of fatherhood, the foundation of it being the act of fatherhood which was done by the former and received by the latter.

From the preceding, we may try to work out **conditions for a relation to be real**. These are **four**: (a) A real distinction between the subject and term. Unless this were so the linking of the two would only be a logical one and not a real one.[1] (b) a subsisting subject, i.e. The one which is to be the source of

1 It may be noted that a real distinction doesn't mean that one can be separated from the other, physically, and they can be made to stand apart form each other, as it were, side by side: it just means that one is not the other nor is part of the other. For instance, existence and essence are really distinct since one is not the other, though they can't be separated

the link should be a complete being, existing in itself, (c) A subsisting term, i.e. that to which the relation is referred must equally be a complete being existing in itself, (d) an immediate foundation, else the subject would not be able to communicate its reality to the relation: in which case, it would have to be the mind of someone or the other who attributes the linking to the other and this would make it a logical relation. In the case of a real relation the mind *discovers* the link between the two; in a logical relation, the mind *creates* the link.

Some clarificatory examples as regards logical relations would be, doubtless, very helpful here. The relationship between a person to be born in the year 2000 and his/her son who might be born in the year 2020 is a logical one. Here, the subject is not a real entity, existing independently of someone's mind. Or, if I compare what others think of me to my own understanding of myself, this is not a real relationship because we do not have two distinct subsisting realities to relate to each other: in each case, it is the same total being which is referred back to itself. Finally, the book that "is known" by me is logically related to me for there is no real change in the book to give a real basis for linking it back to me; the basis for the relation (its foundation, as we have called it) is a real action that has brought about a real change in me only.

Conclusions

Though we have maintained that some relations are real, i.e. they do link certain beings to each other, whether our mind perceives this or not, we have not jumped to the conclusion that every relation is of the real order. Thus, the world we live in is *not* a disconnected heap of isolated existents: there is a real bonding between them, a harmonious integral unity. Were we to uncritically uphold that each and every relation is something real, then we'd find ourselves in an "infinite regress" problem. For instance, there is a real relation between my father and me and the foundation for this is the act of generation which is intrinsic to my father. But there is, obviously, a further relation between the subject (my father) and its immediate foundation (his act of generation, as opposed to some other father's). If I want to say that all relations are real, then I would have to say that there is a real relation between the subject and its foundation. This would requite me to look for the foundation of relation which, according to my assumption, would also have to be real (since I had held that all relations are real). Thus, in order to give a solid foundation to the relation of fatherhood, I would find myself trapped in an infinite, never-ending search for foundations. Thus, the relation would never really get off the ground and so I would have to admit in the end that relations are not real, are only mental fabrications, illusions of the mind and nothing more. Indeed, this

---

from each other, cut apart. But there is only a logical distinction between a human being and his/her act of existence, for the latter is part of the total human person.

is precisely how Bradley argued in favour of his monism! But if we allow for logical relations (that is, some relations are *not* real), then there is no problem. We would say that there is a real relation between my father and me, on account of the immediate foundation of his act of fatherhood. But the relation between him and his act of fatherhood would not be a real relation (for not two distinct and real beings are involved): it is just "in our minds" (a logical relation). So we escape the "infinite regress" pit-fall! As relations between persons involving knowledge of each other and leading up to love and friendship are real, it is no illusion to feel united to those who are separated from us by miles and oceans (even by death). Inasmuch as it is something real that links us together, we are really in union. From this it follows that presence is more than mere physical juxtaposition. I may be physically in proximity with a nigh suffocating group of people, jammed about me, in one of our famous "Bombay locals". But that doesn't make them really "present to" me. On the contrary, I may be physically distanced from some loved one by whole continents (or even death!), yet they are really "present to" me and always will be so, as long as our love or friendship doesn't cease.

Just as we often "keep time" by extrinsic denomination, i.e. we measure succession in a being by reference to the movement of another being (most commonly the sun), so also we often refer to a person or a thing "by extrinsic denomination", that is, by relating it/him/her to some other thing with which some external link has been noticed. Thus I describe someone as "a Puneite" or a "Bombaywallah", designating that person by reference (relation) to his/her place of birth or residence. Or I may identify a stranger in a crowd by calling him "the chap wearing an orange *kurta* and dark glasses", using his relation with these objects to designate him. Relations, therefore, do function in our lives with great practical relevance. However, let us note that we are naming a person not by what he is, but by what he has. Gabriel Marcel has condemned our tendency to identify a person with his function – bus conductor, shop keeper and so on. This involves, he reminds us, reducing a person to the level of a thing (his functional "use" for us) and leads us to treating him/her not as a person but as a thing to be used. It is not surprising that he/she returns us the compliment!

The Christian doctrine of the Trinity, as we all well know, has traditionally followed the Thomistic approach of trying to humbly enter into the mystery using the Scholastic (Aristotelian!) doctrines of relation and of the person (just as the Aristotelian notions of substance and accidents were employed to grasp the mystery of the Eucharist by means of transsubstantiation). However, it might be better nowadays to seek a more personalist route into the heart of this very relevant and dynamic truth. Indeed, we live in a less rationally-dominated, less Hellenistic world and it would be probably more in keeping with the Semitic, biblical (and oriental!) mentality and culture to seek an insight to this revelation along the lines of the philosophy of inter personal relationships and love. We will sketch out such an approach at the end of the next section, appropriately on the person.

d. Towards a "Metaphysics of Love"[2]

Before going to the study of person, it may be attempted to establish a metaphysics of love, though it does not come directly under relations. Love cannot be taken as a secondary aspect of relations. Still this attempt to give a metaphysical basis to love could be taken up within the wider horizon of relations.

First an existential and metaphysical analysis of the human situation and then that of love. Here we encounter both the tragic and the ecstatic aspects of human life.

The human being is a paradox in being. "Perpetually falling into nothing, glowering from without and erupting as a hideous void from within (human being) nonetheless fails to achieve (his/her) own failure."[3] Although everything within and without us cries out for the annihilation of our beings, we do not cease to be. We die, but we never experience our own death. What lies in and beyond death lies beyond our history. Thus strictly speaking, death hides itself from our philosophical experience. So the best we can do is as suggested by Wilhelmsen to insist that an existential analysis points up "the intolerable and yet curiously bracing truth"[4] that the human being is forever threatened by annihilation and yet never is fully annihilated, is forever menaced by non-being and yet continues his/her existence.

In experiencing the possibility of their own non-being as the crucial enemy of their own beings, human beings sense their finiteness and through the finiteness their own transcendence. As a constant seeker, the human person opens the doors to new vistas, each of which leads to nowhere. S/he opens more doors, looks for more possibilities and ventures into unknown areas. S/he may not do anything more than "hang on grimly to the shadow of [her/] his being, as do those pitiful wrecks of humanity who populate our asylums, driven there by anxiety, haunted by the spectre of the facelessness and silence of non-being."[5] Even they continue to be, though threatened and faceless. This insecurity of one's impending non-being cannot be tolerated by us for long. So we try to transcend even our transcendence.

---

2 This section is a modified summary by the editor of F.D. Wilhelmsen, *The Metaphysics of Love*, Sheed and Ward, New York, 1962. 3-50. See also J.F. Kavanaugh, *Human Realisation*, Corpus Books, Cleveland, 1970, 115-118.

3 Wilhelmsen, 19.

4 Ibid.

5 Ibid, 20.

Things around us are finite and limited and contingent. But we are driven both to face the finiteness and attempt to shake off its sting. Scratching forever in the soil of being, our race is destined to track down a place within which humanity can take root and there flourish within the shadow of the absolute. We demand a certain and non-failing ground of being. Humanity makes the demand but not in the sense that the absolute is commanded by the demand; were it so, the facts marshalled above would be illusory; we would have found a more comfortable world than the one we are living in. We demand the absolute as the term of our own transcending – the term is not "dragooned into obedience" by the call of human beings. There is search for the absolute in this sense that the our being is a being-towards-being, finiteness tending to the infinite, a thirsting for immortal life, desirous of God or a restless soul finding its fulfilment only in the infinite.

Thus the tragic sense of life encounters the ecstatic. "Falling into nothing even while (we) strive to be, experiencing (ourselves) essentially as ontological poverty, we nonetheless must give of (ourselves) to the world of things and most especially to the world of persons."[6] Thus the being of the human being is structurally and constitutively a being with others. In the first place this is revealed in communication, which is a need to share meaning and significance with others, in care, which is "the contingent watch over the contingent". The ecstatic drive in us reaches its culmination in love. When we love, our being is realised as a being-for-another. The loves lives literally in the being of the beloved. This is the metaphysics dormant in the beautiful English phrase, "being in love".

An analysis of the negation of love shows that love is an authentic human experience, that the being of ourselves is achieved and realised only in love and that therefore the being of ours is structurally open to love. The negation of love is a self-destroying experience, just like the negations of care and concern. "If love is the free gift of the person to another person, the opposite of love is the attempt to appropriate the being of another to oneself."[7] At the root of every such appropriation there is the human drive to conquer our own indigence, to overcome our own ontological emptiness. Experiencing ourselves as limited and contingent inauthentic human persons try to make up for it by a gathering into their being the being of others. When we scrutinise this process carefully we observe that it involves a "vicious contradiction, a metaphysical violation". Attempting to make the being of another a being for oneself in order that one might fill up what is lacking in one's own being-for-the-appropriated. Thus it is common knowledge that the miser begins first by relating himself to money and ends by being defined by the very money he has

6 Kavanaugh, 116-117.

7 Wilhelmsen, 21-22.

appropriated; thus metaphysically he has become "*a being-for-money*".[8] His own conquest enslaves him. This shows us the irony involved in the failure to respect the irreducibility and the dignity of the being of another thing or person. Every attempt to make another's being exclusively a *being-for-me* ends in my making my being a being-for-that-other. Thus appropriation of another being becomes a self-defeating experience. Ontological poverty is not overcome but accentuated by such an appropriation.

The ecstatic and the tragic meet in a paradox which is one with the very being of human beings. The desire to give and the desire to be fulfilled, the desire to throw myself and the need to be sheltered go hand in hand. Logically though they are opposed, existentially they are the being of human beings. This implies metaphysically that the human being is not a complete person until one has been in love and by the act of a person to whom (one) can give (oneself) freely and who will freely give (one) – rather be for one – the anchor in being that (human being) so desperately needs."[9]

Participation and communication leading to communion is the source of completion for humanity. This is the ultimate experience of love towards which we long for. Thus, we can assert metaphysically that personality is constituted not merely by the "I" but also by the "we".

8 To illustrate this phenomenon, one can imagine that the passive voice of "I own a Ford car" could be "A Ford car owns me". Though not correct grammatically, existentially it is.

9 Kavanaugh, 118.

Chapter 7

The Person

Among the various kinds of beings we come across in the world, persons call for special attention. What is a person? Why is a person an "end in itself." A very relevant issue, indeed!

a. The Issue(s)

As we look around us we see in this world a great variety of beings. A random list, cited by the Wallrus and the Carpenter in *Alice in Wonderland*, includes "shoes and ships and sealing-wax and cabbages and kings". This is quite a representative list: it includes human artefacts (manufactured articles put together by human beings), living beings and, among these, one of the vegetative order (cabbages) and one of the rational and human level (kings). What is missing from the catalogue is a representative of the mineral kingdom (water, iron, oxygen) and of the animal world (which would include also insects, fish and reptiles). After having emphasised first of all (very deliberately!) the essential interconnectedness and unity of all beings (through those relations which are real and objective, albeit "the weakest of all beings"), we now focus on the various kinds of beings that populate our cosmos. Some beings – most obviously artefacts – are really not one single and integral reality but an aggregate of individual beings, held together artificially and easily dismantle able. The so called "mineral kingdom" (comprising non-living beings found freely in nature) can easily be broken up or separated without any radical change appearing in the process: we can break up a piece of iron ore into smaller bits, or draw a bucket of water from a mighty reservoir. However, were we to attempt doing so to a living being – "cut off" a part of it – the being would, in various degrees, be impaired, a natural process of repair would be set in motion and the amputated part would corrupt. It is clear, then, that there is a greater level of unity in a living, organic being than in an inorganic one. Furthermore, among living beings, there is a special category that seems to stand out and merit particular attention and respect: the person. It has taken us a long time to recognise that all human beings are persons: blacks, women and even "gays"! It is only recently that we have begun to speak of respecting the rights of animals and of the environment, too. A belated recognition of the integral wholeness of reality has been forced upon us by recent developments in ecology. In this section, then, we take a look at this variety within beings, as such. In particular we will pay attention to the person: what is a person? What is required for a being to be hailed as a person? Why should a person be given special treatment and treated, like Kant said, "as an end in oneself"? The practical, pastoral implications of these and similar questions can hardly be exaggerated.

b. "Supposites" and "principles of being"

If a deft-fingered pickpocket is arrested, he could hardly claim that it was his "naughty fingers" that were to blame and not he! True, his fingers were immediately and directly responsible for his crime, but they have no capacity to act freely on their own. Thus, we arrive at the notion of an ultimate source of responsibility or imputability for an action, in this case, the thief, the one who freely chose to use his fingers to steal. So we come to the notions of the supposite (in our example, the thief) and the principle of being (his fingers). However, supposites are not only free beings who are personally responsible for their actions. A supposite could be any being (free or not) which has initiated an action. Hence, we could say that the moon is the supposite involved in bringing about the ebb and flow of the tides. The Latin word *sup-positum* means "the one placed under", i.e. the one underlying a being's activities.

Let us now try to work out a more precise philosophical definition of a supposite. In the first place, "supposite" is a barbarous word in English. It might be better to use a phrase like "individual being" or something like that – as Fr. De Marneffe sj does in his notes on *Metaphysics.*[1] Scholastics have traditionally assembled four necessary qualities for a being to be ranked as an authentic "supposite" or individual being. If an entity doesn't possess all four of these qualities, it is to be classed as a "principle of being".

Conditions for being a "supposite" (a). **Subsistence**: It must exist "in itself" and not derive its existence by "inherence in another" (like an accident or additive, as we prefer to say). This of course, does not rule out the possibility of having received its proper act of existence from another (i.e.

1 Pune: JDV and Barrackpore: Morning Star 1986.

God), participating in Him (not inhering in Him: it's not that God and the creature share the same act of existence among themselves).

(b) **Distinctness**: By this we mean that it is not identical with another being nor even a part of it. Creatures are supposites, for their participation in God does not render them identical with God or parts of God – unless we uphold some kind of pantheistic conception of reality. Again I may be "similar to" other human beings, I may even be "the spitting image" of my twin brother, such that strangers might not be able to tell us apart, but I am not my brother for all that: we are two distinct realities.

(c) **Wholeness**: In other words, a certain completeness in the development of the being is necessary. A grown, physically mature adult human being is a "whole" man or woman. This, of course, does not mean that there cannot be further scope for dynamic development. The man or woman in question can grow in wisdom or the capacity to love. But the arms or legs of the individual concerned are not "whole beings": they are part of the wholeness of the person in question.

(d) **A certain nature**: A supposite must have a certain basic unity in its properties and actions and this must flow from within, not something that results from construction and programming from outside, as in the case of a computer (which, as we shall see, is in reality only an aggregate). If this nature is rational we call the supposite a person.

c. Aggregates

But before we pass on to the person, the key issue of this chapter, let us pause for a moment to consider what we may call aggregates. These are, strictly speaking, not one single being but actually a collection of beings, put together in an orderly way by humans, and held together by artificial bonds. Thus, a typewriter, a car and a ball pen, for instance, are not real supposites but aggregates: they are a clever assemblage of metal and other well-shaped parts, held together by screws, soldering, welding or what not. Humans, animals and plants, on the other hand, are obvious supposites. Their unity of activity arises from within (their nature, the scholastics would say). They come into existence, not by construction (like machines and other manufactured articles) but by birth. They have within them an inner dynamism which seeks their nourishment, repair (in case of injury) and reproduction. Of course, some highly sophisticated computers give evidence of a very high "unity of activity" and are far more efficient than human beings in responding to what appear to be rational challenges. But they are not supposites, let alone persons, for all that. In the first place, they have to be set in motion from outside (unlike human, animals and even plants), they cannot reproduce themselves or really set off a natural "repair-process" when they are damaged. Computer parts can be replaced without much difficulty, whereas amputations and transplants (or "grafts", as we say in the case of plants) are a much more complex operation, having a widespread repercussion on the whole organism and requiring a more or less protracted period of recuperation. Thus the "unity of activity" in a computer is very much attenuated when compared to living things, even the lowest of living things, the plant. That there is a certain "unity in activity" in inorganic substances – minerals, gases, fluids – can be inferred from the unity and distinctness of their properties and activities and these can be seen to "flow from within". So iron obtained anyhow from anywhere always melts at a definite temperature under normal pressure and this is quite distinct from the melting-point of, say copper. Since these are non-living beings, their "unity of activity" is not as integrated as that of living beings and they can be separated or broken up into smaller parts without much difficulty and without any impairment of the original whole or the parts. Thus, I can draw a bucket of water from a lake or break up a piece of iron into smaller bits and the smaller portions will have the same properties as the original larger amount and won't perish on being "cut off" from the "parent" being. It is for scientists to tell us exactly wherein resides the actual individuality of iron or water (at the atomic or molecular level).

d. The PERSON

We have already indicated the traditional scholastic definition of the person: a rational (or, if you prefer, an intellectual) supposite. More in detail, a person is whole, distinct, subsistent of a rational (or intellectual) nature. This is how scholastics in general, and Thomists in particular, define the person. But let us take a brief glance at how this definition evolved.

Etymologically, person comes from the Latin *per-sona* (literally, one through which sounds are made), a mask. The Greek equivalent was *pros pon*. In the classical days of Latin and Greek drama, the characters, instead of make-up, wore type masks, called *personae*. Thus there was the mask of the old man, the hero, the heroine, the villain and so on. In course of time, the word was applied to the character depicted by the one who wore the mask. Eventually it was referred to the actor or actress.

It was Boethius, the 4th century Christian savant and forerunner of scholasticism, who gave us the definition of person as "an individual substance of a rational nature."[2] Aquinas slightly revised this and put it down as "distinct subsistence of a rational nature."[3] The reason why he sought to link up person with subsistence, rather than substance, was because he wanted to use the related (but not identical) concepts of substance and person to throw light on the mystery of the Trinity. The Gospels and Epistles tell us that God is somehow one and somehow three: of course, it would be totally against the

2 cited by Aquinas in ST 1, 29, 1.

3 Ibid.

principle of identity and contradiction were we to interpret this to mean that God is one and three at the same time and under the same aspect! So he held that God, in His/Her most basic and underlying aspect (as substance) is one and from a less basic dimension, that of subsistence, He/She is three and each of these is a person, a personal being, among other things, an ultimate centre of attribution (i.e. it is the **person** who acts, who is responsible for what is done, not his/her faculties or organs). Thus in God, there are three distinct agents, as it were: it is the Second Person who became incarnate and died for us, rising again and leading us to the Father. It is not the Father or the Spirit who did these things: they are different persons and are responsible for other salvific acts.

Aquinas stressed the role of reason or the intellect in personhood, giving pride of place to that spiritual faculty in the Scholastic perspective. Hence the "intellectualism of St.Thomas". However, other scholastics, notably his mentor and co-Dominican, St.Albert (revered as "the Great") preferred to underscore the priority of the will in all things: he is called a "voluntarist" or a "volitionist". Not that there is any real contradiction in their views. The one emphasises the initially perfective act of the person (the intellect), the other the completive dimension of personhood (love, the act of the will). If Aquinas sees the beatific vision as primarily an act of the intellect and Albert as essentially an act of the will, they are reminding us of the scholastic adage that they both uphold, "The will follows the intellect." Aquinas is underscoring the spiritual faculty that leads and Albert is pointing out that the one that follows bringing full flowering to the activity initiated by the former. After all, you can't love someone whom you don't know, but, in a personal relationship, knowledge is fundamentally a drive which is meant to end in love.

I am more inclined to go along with St. Albert than St. Thomas and define the person as a being capable of loving and of being loved. Of course, such a person would have to be an intellectual supposite – that is implied by the very definition itself, for there can be no love of what is totally unknown (hence, a person must be capable of knowing): the will and its acts follow the intellect. Inasmuch as the will is blind, there must be a precedent intellectual act to stir it to action. I would rather put the emphasis on loving, rather than knowledge as the latter approach is more consonant with Greek thinking and the former is more in keeping with the biblical viewpoint. If Aristotle defined God as *neoesis noeseos* (literally, "thought thinking about itself"), St. John called God love. Thought is essentially an inward movement, intussusceptation (drawing things into oneself and making things what one is). Hence the traditional synonym for God as the Absolute (literally, the one cut off from), the unrelated. To call God love is an extremely radical, revolutionary idea: love, by definition is just the opposite of the absolute, unrelated, self-withdrawn reality.

By its very nature, love is turned to others, is related, is a movement away from self. Thus a person is fully a person not when he or she is cogitating in isolation and making things one with itself through the intellect, but when, Godlike, he/she is reaching out to others, entering into their lives and beings through love. This is what the incarnation is all about and we human persons would do well to remember that. Our perfection is not in withdrawal. If we wish to be God like, we have to be outgoing, community persons and not cold "Absolutes", unmoved and locked up in ourselves! Maybe Aquinas' approach is not really opposed to all this but it is far easier to misunderstand this way and end up in precisely that conception of the person!

e. Persons as "ends in themselves"

Though it was Immanuel Kant who popularised the idea that persons are ends in themselves and can never be used "merely as a means", the view had been upheld a long time before him (notably by scholastic thinkers). A means is that which is useful, a thing (and the word is deliberately chosen) which is sought only for the sake of something else and not desired for its own sake. Thus as long as I need my cycle or my tooth brush it is of any value for me: once I've finished using it, I put it aside and forget about it. Persons are not things: they are to be loved, not used. Of course, there are occasions when I make use of a person (his or her services, to be precise), as when I ask someone to drop me to the station by motor-bike or even when I avail of a driver and bus conductor to use the public transport. Kant recognised that we sometimes have to "make use of" each other's services: that is why he, very wisely, said we shouldn't use a person *merely* as a means. We need make use of people's services from time to time. That is what life in community is all about: mutual co-operation and assistance. But it would be totally wrong on my part were I to use a person merely as a means, exactly like I would use, say my toothbrush or cycle. I must respect the freedom of the person and politely request his/her services, recognising his/her right to refuse. I have to pay him or her some compensation if he or she is a public servant like a bus driver (this is done by paying for my ticket.) Finally, I must render to him or her the basic respect that is due to a person, something which I am in no wise obliged to give to my cycle or toothbrush. We may find ourselves in a situation where we have to use the other person as a means, but nothing would justify us using him or her merely as a means!

But why not? What is the basic metaphysical reason as to why we cannot, should not use a person merely as a means? On what grounds can persons claim preferential treatment over things? There is a very good reason for this. And humanists, of both the theistic as well as the atheistic persuasions, would uphold it.

For theistic humanists, the person is an "end in himself/herself" because, of all created beings only the person can directly attain the ultimate end of all reality. Our transcendental analysis of the metaphysical fact of direct judgement has revealed that the unlimited being is the ultimate goal of my intellectual dynamism, the dynamism that underlies all my other striving and drives. Inasmuch as I can know and love, I can directly apprehend (not comprehend) the ultimate reality though, in this present condition, I can only do so indirectly and mediately: here and now I have only a mediated encounter with the Unlimited Being (i.e. through the finite things which I affirm in my daily experience). But I could – if that opportunity were granted me as a freely bestowed gift (in the beatific vision, for instance) – respond directly to such a direct, personal encounter by means of my "spiritual" faculties. Other, non-personal beings, can attain the ultimate and of all reality only in and through personal beings like myself. Hence it is that other beings can be sought and used merely as a means whereas persons can never be so exploited. Let us remember that an "end in oneself" is not the same as the ultimate end. No finite person can be made one's ultimate end, though he or she must be loved for his or her own sake and not even be "used spiritually" (whatever that is supposed to imply) as a means to attain God. If there comes about a clash between any person I love and God (a clash of loyalties or demands) then, without ceasing to love the former, I have to elicit preferential love for the latter, i.e. God. Let us also not forget that to make any finite person my ultimate end would be to do him or her grievous harm. For I would be absolutising or divinising him or her. This would be unfair and tantamount to making demands of him or her that he or she would be unable to fulfil!

The **atheistic humanist** would agree that a person is an end in him/herself, though for a different reason. The argument would be that there is no higher being given us on earth than the human person. Only humans have consciousness to the extent of being free, intelligent and creative. Only human beings can love each other in the fullest sense of the term. Hence they cannot be treated as mere things, as inanimate or non-free, non-rational beings. Indeed, some of the most ardent and dedicated champions of human rights have been atheists who have been prepared to die for their fellowmen and women... and have actually done so. There do exist even martyrs of love among Marxists!

f. Societies

Just as collections of things can be gathered together into aggregates and held together by some external means and thereby, thanks to the creativeness and inventiveness of human beings, be put to work to fulfil various uses, persons, too, can form analogous groupings or societies. The basic difference here is that such persons have come together freely and bind themselves together by moral (not physical) links, which they can surrender if and when they so will.

Such groups may come together for a limited goal (e.g. to perfect their skills in a particular language or sport: thus we have language academies and sports "clubs") or in an attempt to support and help each other in all-round personal growth and development (as may be the case in a nation, a religious order or a religion). The scholastics generally referred to the last group as "perfect" societies and the former as "imperfect" societies. The appellation "perfect" or "imperfect" was not meant to refer to the moral status of the persons who made up the society in question! In the first place, *perfecta* in Latin means complete and, in the second place, it is meant to be descriptive of the goal of the society. A "perfect" society is one which seeks the total, all-round good of the persons who are its members. In that sense, a religion is most adequately called a perfect society, inasmuch as it seeks to make persons better persons and not just better speakers or better citizens or better athletes.

A very relevant question which is often asked today is, to what extent can a society (club, the state, a religion) ask the individual to sacrifice himself or herself for the common good? It is equally clear that we cannot allow a person to be swallowed up and annihilated, as it were, by any society: he or she is an end in itself and can't be totally sacrificed for some other allegedly "higher purpose". But persons are no mere private individuals: a person is a "community being", too. After all, the supremely perfective acts of a person are knowing and loving and these turn one outside of himself/herself – indeed, as we have seen, both these "spiritual" activities attain their fulfilment in an interpersonal relationship. So, were a person to refuse to relate himself to others in a meaningful community he would frustrate one of the most essential dimensions of his being. Hence, we cannot advocate the "drop out" solution, where a person turns his back on society, on all societies and refuses to make any adjustments or sacrifices for the community. But where do we draw the line?

Generally speaking, no society can use a person **merely** as a means. If a given society were to ask a person to do something immoral for the sake of an alleged "greater good", it would be wrong. For instance, if a given society decided to eliminate all "unproductive" persons (the aged, the terminally ill and the mentally defective) on the grounds that, since they were not making any contribution to the per capita income of the people and were, on the contrary, a drain on its resources, obviously this would be treating all those persons as mere means for augmenting the income of society (even if this did, in the long run, increase the apparent well-being of the others – but, can one really become an all-round better person by forcibly killing of hopeless and helpless people who might have already given their best to society or who, through no fault of their own, cannot contribute to the amount of goods and services that society craves? Besides, even if they are not "productive" in this narrow, physical sense, can we be so sure that they are unable to contribute to the personal growth of people in other, more vital, ways?). So also would it be against the personal nature of humans, to take children away from their families and indoctrinate them in isolation from their natural parents and families. Again, it would be totally false to identify personhood with a particular ethnic origin or social class or even sex or the colour of ones skin. We have seen that what constitutes a person is something deeper than any of these things.

This does not deny the fact that sometimes, for a limited period, the state may curtail some personal rights for the sake of the deprived, in order to give them a chance to overcome the obstacles and injustices meted out to them by an unfair and dominant class. Hence the reservation quotas and land ceilings may interfere with the legitimate aspirations of certain persons, but these are temporary and seek to right an unjustified imbalance that has been done in the past. In all these matters, there needs to be a place for dialogue and the accepted process of democracy. People have also the right to protest decisions of the State if they feel, in good conscience, that these go against fundamental personal rights but they should be on the guard against ways and means of protesting that are uncalled for, such as hasty resort of violence and endangering lives of innocent and helpless people. In the Optional on *Hunger and Violence*[4] we will have occasion to discuss whether and under what conditions people may resort to violence. Of course, there ever remains the possibility of an individual or a group freely sacrificing themselves for the good of their fellows, but one cannot oblige them to do so. Even in case of war, conscription must give way to honest conscientious objectors, giving them non-combative roles and duties which, in effect, may be as vital, demanding and daring as that of active soldiers.

g. Human rights

On December 10, 1948, the United Nations General Assembly adopted the Declaration of Universal Rights. In general, this recognises that all persons are equal in dignity and rights, and went on to list some of these latter as the right to life, liberty and security. Among the other rights that are more specifically spelt out in national constitutions are the right to information, religion, speech, press and assembly. Of course, in times of emergency – such as war or natural calamities (earth-quakes, floods etc.), the State has a right to impose a temporary ban on some of these rights in order to prevent a worsening of an unusually disturbed situation. But, as was mentioned before, these can only be temporary and there should be due reason for such drastic measures. It does not reflect very highly on human history that, in spite of the above declaration, there had to be an UN Commission of the Status of Women and, in our times, a Declaration on the Rights of the Child has to be drawn up and passed (are women and children sub-human beings, thereby escaping the

4 Cf. JDV, Pune.

purview of the 1948 Declaration?). It is interesting to know that although most nations in the world have granted female suffrage, as it is called, the tiny state of Leichtenstein (population 30,000), boarding Austria, voted in 1971 against granting the vote to women, thereby earning for itself the dubious reputation of being the only European nation that does not allow women the vote! As for the Rights of the Child, to mention a few, there is the right to a happy childhood and to name and nationality from birth. Besides, there is the right to parental love and understanding, adequate education, pre-natal and post-natal care, medical assistance, to full opportunities for play and recreation as well as to be the first to receive help in times of disaster.

We have also come to realise that though animals, inasmuch as they are not persons, cannot be strictly said to have rights. Still cruelty to them on any grounds would be unjustified (even if tastier food and more high-quality cosmetics could result): among other things, this hardens and dehumanises persons who make themselves impervious to the agony of these helpless creatures. Finally, the ecological movement and the sense of our solidarity with the whole cosmos has led us to recognise that, in a sense, the natural environment has certain rights too, the disregard of which will only redound to our disease.

h. God as personal

We are all familiar with the controversy, in traditional Hindu thinking, about God as *nirguna* and *saguna* (erroneously translated as impersonal and personal), the former representing a higher and more enlightened conception of the Absolute. However, as we now realise, the terms should more accurately be rendered as "without attributes" and "with attributes" respectively. In other words, Indian thinkers are certainly not rejecting the idea that the Brahman be incapable of knowing or loving. Rather, they are rejecting an overly anthropomorphic understanding of God, one in which the Absolute is thought to be a person just as we are persons, with all the human limitations of personhood (embodiedness, jealousy, possessiveness and so on), not to mention the various distinctions that would militate against the divine simplicity (=absence of parts). Indeed, the Brahman is *sat-cit-Œnanda* (being-consciousness-bliss) and these are very markedly personalist qualities. However, in order to avoid misunderstandings, it might be better to say that, in the Christian conception, God is personal, rather than say that God is a person (that careless indefinite article would rank God along with the various human persons, all on the same level). To say that God is personal, on the other hand, would merely imply that he is a being who is capable of loving and being loved (or an intellectual supposite, if one prefers the more traditional definition), without suggesting that God's way of knowing and loving (and, therefore, of being a person) is on a par with ours! In other words, we are emphasising the fact that we are using the word, person, analogically.

Again, many of our contemporaries – especially youth – say that they'd rather speak of God "as a force" than as a person. It seems to be that this is the result of a gross misunderstanding. No doubt, the reference to force is in order to bring out the dynamism at the heart of the divinity, as well as the power and drive (energy?) that is communicated thereby to all creatures as, for instance, a power station distributes electrical energy to all appliances that are "plugged in". This is, indeed, a valuable analogy and may well serve to correct the traditionally static understanding of God that some of us have inherited. But a force, however powerful (think of the force of gravity, or a magnetic field or even nuclear fission), for all its awesome might, remains unconscious and quite incapable of loving or being loved. Would it not be better to revise our, perhaps overly static understanding of person, reminding ourselves that all beings are dynamic and that personal beings are the most dynamic of all? No analogy is perfect but, in the long run, the image of force is probably a good deal poorer than that of the person.

i. Historical development of "person"

Etymology aside, there is no commonly accepted usage of the term in common speech. In general, "person" is a word used to refer to human beings and "thing" is the general term for all other objects of our experience. It is at least, an implicit acknowledgement that human beings are entitled to special treatment and cannot be dealt with on a par with sub-human reality.

French philosophers at the turn of this century focused on the human person and we are all familiar with Emmanuel Mounier who consciously founded a school of thought called "personalism".[5] He felt that the two other "personalist" philosophies of his time, Marxism and Existentialism were inadequate: the former did not respect the individual dignity of the person sufficiently, sacrificing him/her to the totalitarian state and the latter, under the influence of Sartre, was moving towards atheism. Authentic personalism, he felt, had to respect the personal dignity and freedom of each individual man and woman, while not denying his or her social responsibility and it is only within a theistic world-view that the person's greatness and uniqueness can be safe-guarded.

If existentialism tended to move towards the opposite extreme, stressing individual freedom to the extent of almost leading one to despise society (ˆ *la* Kierkegaard), thinkers like Marcel sought to restore the balance. But perhaps the whole of history will continue to be the tale of the dialectic between the person as individual and the person as community-oriented and of how the see-saw slopes precariously now one way, now another.

---

5 cf. his *A Personalist Manifesto* and *Le Personalisme*, published in 1936 and 1950 respectively at Paris.

Chapter 8

Causality

We have already established the metaphysical principle of causality with Maréchal; here we take a closer look at the various kinds of causality at work in the world.

a. The fundamental issues

Having studied the variety of material beings and noted that not just no person, but no being, is an island (there is a certain interconnectedness in the cosmos), we pass on to a more detailed study of just how these beings interact. We have already, thanks to Marechal, responded to Hume's critique of both metaphysical and empirical causality and there is no need to retrace ground already covered. Apart from taking a closer look at the different kind of causes that there are, we shall tie up a few loose ends from various areas.

b. The contemporary scene

It would indicate a nigh culpable blindness on our part were we to simply pass over in silence that many contemporary thinkers regard causality as "the most treacherous concept that man has fabricated to interpret his experiences in the physical world."[1] J. Loewenberg sums up the discussion in a more balanced way, saying:

While all agree that there is something opaque about the idea of causality, its darkness has been accounted for in different ways, some ascribing it to

1 Herold Brown, "Causality and the Cosmos", in *Causality*, edited by George P.Adams et al., Berkeley, Univ. of California Press, 1932, 41.

profundity, some to confusion, others to mystery. No wonder, then, that in some quarters causality has assumed the character of a *bête noire*.[2]

There seem to be two reasons why causality gets such bad press from many of today's thinkers. The first is that it is seen as primarily the invention of Aristotle, from whose domination (and oft crippling) effects modern science has long broken away. The later alliance of the Stagyrite's thought with Christian philosophy and theology did not help the situation either. Bertrand Russell, for reasons such as these, dismissed causality as one of the "relics of a bygone age" and there are others who keep on reminding us that the concept seldom figures in the vocabulary of contemporary physicists.

The other objection is as old as Hume and it boils down to a charge of rank anthropocentrism. As the man who woke Kant from his alleged "dogmatic slumber" put it:

Necessity [i.e. the necessary cause-effect link] is ... nothing but an internal impression of the mind, or a determination to carry our thoughts from one object to another.... The efficacy or energy of causes is neither [to be] placed in the causes themselves nor in the deity nor in the concurrence of these two principles; but belongs entirely to the soul [i.e. mind], which considers the union of two or more objects of all past instances. 'Tis here that the real power of causes is placed, along with their connection and necessity. [3]

We might read these (and similar) words as a reminder to us that there are certain complex metaphysical issues related to the notion of causality and that we should be on our guard against naïve and glib assumptions. However, as I have mentioned above, we have already had occasion to reply to these difficulties ad there is no need to take up the issue once more.

Let us point out also that it is premature, futile and ridiculous to try and outlaw all discussions on causality from our life. In the first place, law and jurisprudence would be thwarted of their very purpose if it were forbidden to seek the cause of violent death, fire and accidents. Public health and medical research would have to put a stop to their efforts to find out the cause (and thereby, the remedy) for infectious diseases. Historians and journalists would not be able to speculate about the causes of the World War II or Indira Gandhi's assasination. Indeed, if we were to veto all exchanges which, implicitly or explicitly, directly or indirectly, spoke of causes and effects, there would be precious little left to say – or do. As John Wild, tellingly observes, "No one who really believed in causal efficiency would ever read a detective story."[4]

2 "The Elasticity of the Idea of Causality," Ibid, 3

3 *A Treatise of Human Nature*, I, part 3, section 14

4 "Realistic Defence of Causal Efficacy", in *Review of Metaphysics*, 2, June 1949.

c. General definition of cause

It is common knowledge that Aristotle distinguished four kinds of causes, two being extrinsic and two intrinsic. However, he made no claims for originality in this regard. He readily enough admitted that his predecessors had in general treated of all four but criticised them for emphasising some to the neglect of the others. The Milesians, for instance, were too preoccupied with finding the basic stuff out of which the things of our experience was made (the *archã*, in effect, the material cause of the cosmos). The atomist, Empedocles, drew attention to efficient causality (poetically called love and strife, as the two motivating factors in evolution) and left it at that. Plato, on the other hand, thought it was vital to concentrate on the forms of all things (formal causes). Aristotle was convinced that all these approaches were far too narrow.

Cause, in general as it underlies all the various types outlined above, could be defined, in Aristotelian terms as "*that which influences the being of another.*" The **effect** would be that which results from the above-mentioned influence. The exact nature of the influence depends on the type of causality in question. Sometimes the effect may be simultaneous with the cause: I am a human being (effect) as long as my "soul" (formal cause) is in me. Sometimes there is a temporal priority of cause over effect: I kick the ball (efficient cause) and a goal results (effect). As may be noticed, the former is an instance of an intrinsic cause at work, the latter exemplifies extrinsic causality. In the Aristotelian scheme, there are two broad sub divisions of causality, each of which, as we shall see, consisting of two kinds.

Intrinsic causes comprise those which are part of the effect hence the name 'intrinsic'. There are two such: (a) the *formal cause*, which specifies the effect. Thus the human and canine "souls" are the formal cause of a human being and a dog, respectively; (b) the *material cause*: that out of which the effect is made. Thus wood is the material cause of the table and various pieces of metal and glass, fitted together, are the material cause of my spectacles.

Extrinsic causes on the other hand, are and remain – completely distinct (separate) from the effect. Thus we have the *efficient cause*, which "makes the effect come into existence either totally or partially". God is the **efficient** cause of the world and the carpenter is the efficient cause of the table. God, however, is responsible for the total being of the world: he brought it into existence out of nothingness, i.e., out of no pre-existing raw material. But the carpenter is not responsible for the totality of the table in that sense: he works on pre-existing raw material. His efficient causality consists in giving a new shape to the wood. Then there is the *final cause*, the reason for which something is done. It may not exist yet, as such. But, at least as an "anticipated good" it attracts or influences a being to act. Thus, an athlete trains in order to win a prize or a criminal murders for the purpose of revenge or to steal money.

Let us now explore the variety of final and efficient causes and then distinguish genuine causes from those which are not proper causes at all, but are often mistakenly assumed to be so.

d. Varieties of FINAL causes

Another common name for a final cause is "end". We can, first of all, divide up final causes or ends according to their reference. Under this heading, we can distinguish three instances of this: (a) the objective final cause or end, that is, the object which attracts the agent: e.g. a person wants to build a house or a chair. (b) the subjective final cause or end – the quality or perfection that is sought to be realised in the agent through attainment of the objective end: e.g. the comfort or pleasure in having it. (c) the altruistic final cause or end: this refers to other persons who would directly or indirectly profit from the agent's obtaining the objective end e.g. his family, who will also enjoy the house he has built. As a result of having a nice house, he will be happy and will be able to serve his customers better. So, customer's good-will could also be listed as an altruistic end of his building a nice house. However, it is not so "altruistic" as the first example, as he seeks to please his customers for his own benefit (more business)!

Sometimes it is more feasible to sub-divide final causes according to their degree of subordination. This happens when it is relevant to recognise that an action is done in order to obtain something which is necessary to attain some higher goal. For instance, I study philosophy in order to get the Diploma or BPh, so that I will be able to do my theology and finally be ordained a priest. We note how, according to the scholastic axiom, what is first in intention (i.e. uppermost in mind – here, the priesthood) is last in execution (I become a priest after having done my studies in philosophy and theology).

Closely linked to the above occurs also the possibility of viewing ends from the point of view of their importance. Thus we can speak of a mere means, that is, a thing desired, not for its own sake, but solely for the sake of another. If – and as long as – I need to write, I desire a pen or pencil. Once I no longer have need to write, I lose interest in these means. Then there is an intermediary end which is sought or loved for its own sake but which also assists me to attain other ends (though I may not even consciously advert to this last fact). Thus I love a friend for his/her own sake. However, this friend also helps me to attain other ends, such as personal growth and experience of God. Finally, we have the final end, the end which is (consciously or unconsciously) sought beyond all else. This may vary from person to person. For a rank capitalist, money or power would be the ultimate end of all his actions. For a sincere believer, God would be the ultimate end and all other loves, goals and ends would be integrated into this supreme, over-arching inspiration.

Very often, several ends are blended together in one's actions. Often it may not be possible to say which is primary and which is secondary. A violinist may play for personal satisfaction, for making money and for acquiring fame. In the recent debate on contraception, controversy frequently rages about whether production of offspring or the expression of mutual love is the primary goal of the sexual act in marriage (or whether such a question is a relevant one at all!)....

It is good to be aware of these various nuances. Occasionally, especially in complex ethical situations, a lot of light can be shed on a vexing issue if one is able to distinguish and disentangle some of the final causes or ends at work.

e. Varieties of EFFICIENT causes

The first and very relevant distinction here (one that have tremendous relevance in all ethical and moral questions) concerns **co-ordinated** and **sub-ordinated** efficient causality. Sometimes, when a number of efficient causes are at work, they all do so on the same level. This is an instance of co-ordination, as when a number of seminarians are working together in the garden, or a big group of women and men are carrying building materials for constructing, say, a new block in the University of Jnana-Deepa Vidyapeeth, Pune. But, in such cases, there might also be some element of sub-ordination. This happens when one or more workers has precedence over the others, either in time or in importance. The mason has temporal precedence over the construction workers who are sub-ordinate to him and carry out his plans (though he may not even be present at the building site). The head gardener may be working along with his helpers, but the latter are directed by him and follow his instructions. They are subordinate to him who has priority of importance over them. The same would apply to the officers and the *jawans* in the army. This subordination can be further subdivided into two significant types. First, we have *inherent* (sometimes called "vertical") subordination. In this case, all the various causes involved must be active at the same time, else the effect won't follow. For the fan blades to turn the instrument must be switched on and the wires must be connected to the source of power which, in turn, must be continually emitting power. If anyone of the links in this subordinate chain of causes becomes inactive, the fan blades will cease turning. Then there is *accidental* (or "horizontal") subordination, Here the various causes in the series do not have to be "at work" at the same time. They merely "pass on" some influence and my even cease to exist while the influence is passed down the rest of the line. Thus, my great grandparent generated my grand parents who, in turn, gave birth to my parents and I was born of these latter. If it weren't for the earlier efficient causality of my great-grandparents, I would not be alive today. But they might very well have been long dead and gone while my parents were generating me! Hence, the activity of the earlier causes in an accidental series is not necessary for the activity of the later ones to take place (unlike the example of the fan, above). An accidental series of causes may stretch to infinity. It is only an inherent series that rules out infinite regress.[5]

Then we have **principal** and **instrumental** causes. The basic difference between the two is that (apart from divine concurrence) the latter, though it does make some contribution of its own, needs the influence of another cause to act. Obviously, only God is the absolutely principal cause, that is, a cause which requires intervention of no other being in order to act. Any living being would be a relatively principal cause of its vital activity (nourishment, growth etc.): such a cause needs no other power (apart from divine concurrence) to set itself in action. An instrumental cause does make some effective impact on what is produced, but it requires intervention from some other principal cause (God's concurrence besides) in order to act. Thus, as I type these lines, my computer is the instrumental cause and I am the principal cause. The instrument makes a real contribution: left to myself, without any writing instrument, I cannot write at all! Yet, it is I who decide what my computer (or pen or pencil) puts on paper. In other words, it is the principal cause who merits praise or blame for what is done. Notice, however, that the instrumental cause is inanimate, non living and, most important of all, not free, so in no wise responsible for the good or ill or what it helped to effect. Now, though we may piously speak of ourselves as "God's instruments", let us remember that this is, at best, extrinsic analogy. Human beings are not inert, unfree things and cannot be "merely used" by God in the way I "use" my pen. The free collaboration of human persons is required before they can collaborate with God. The old example of the evangelists being the instrumental cause and God the principal cause of the writing of the Scriptures is metaphysically untenable (apart from the other difficulties of accounting for error, contradictions and the intervention of the sociological medium). It might be less misleading to speak of subordinated causes here. If the evangelist remains a free agent, collaborating with God in the writing of the Scriptures, then it is possible to account for traces of human prejudice or of one's cultural conditioning slipping in the way of "inspiration". If one were to hold the totally passive contribution of human instrumentality (apart from the minimal level of "activity" that we see in any tool or piece of equipment we use) then we have to maintain that there can be no critical reading of scripture, no adaptation to new situations – not to mention various other metaphysical difficulties, namely, that God's way of thinking shares in the evident limitations of the sacred writers and so on. Finally, we'd have to admit that God was using persons (the evangelists) "merely as a means" which is grossly immoral and ethical, even if done by God!

5 Cf. The five ways of Aquinas.

Some neo-scholastics[6] introduce a further kind of causality in this regard when speaking of the human contribution to God's infusion of the human soul into the embryonic matter prepared by the action of sperm and ova. They say the human agency amounts to a "dispositive" causality, in the sense that it provides, furnishes or gets the matter ready to receive God's intervening causality. Whatever may be one's response to this way of thinking about conception, this might be a useful way of speaking of the responsibility of the human person as regards the action of God's grace. We can but better dispose or open ourselves to such possibility; we can no way demand, command or call for it as a right!

Sometimes there is a lot of careless talk about *sufficient* and *necessary causes*. Hence, a few precisions in this regard would not be out of order. A sufficient cause would be one which, when it acts, the effect must follow. In this sense, God is the sufficient cause of creation: God is not obliged to create but if he decides to do so then creation inevitably results. When applied to finite beings, we call by the name "sufficient cause" the last one in a series, often forgetting that the so called "sufficient cause" would not be "sufficient in itself" to act if the other links in the chain didn't do their bit. In practice, the entire chain as a whole constitutes the sufficient causality. Thus, we may speak of the hook being the sufficient cause of the fish's being caught. But it was able to act only because it was fixed to the line and the line was manipulated by the fisherman and so on. As for "necessary causes", we need to make a distinction, first, between two ways of understanding the term. In one sense "necessary" means required (the opposite of unnecessary). In other words, it is that which must be there for an effect to take place. Sometimes a substitute may be able to do the job. In that case the particular being is not really necessary. God is clearly the necessary cause of creation and brooks no substitutes (no being other than God can create). For a typed page, a typewriter and a typist are necessary, but only relatively so. The page could after all, be (re-) produced by a Xerox machine! In another sense, "necessary" can mean "not free". In that sense, the law of gravity necessarily causes material beings to fall to the ground: it is not free to either make them fall or float in the air. A free cause, as in the case of a human agent, may or may not act, or could act either in this way or in that! The matter is further complicated by the fact that often, with regard to free (human) causality, we speak of "accidental causes". An accidental cause, in this context, would refer to a cause which produces an effect that was not intentionally willed by the free agent. Thus my carelessness may "accidentally cause" a fire to take place or someone to get injured. Though some eminent authors rank conditions, occasions or qualifying circumstances

6 For example, James Albertson sj, "Instrumental Causality in St. Thomas", *New Scholasticism*, 28 (1954), pp. 409 – 35.

as another types of accidental cause, I would rather not do so. As we shall see, they don't directly contribute to the effect, but rather have some impact on the cause and its activity. Let's take a closer look at these.

f. Conditions, Occasions and Qualifying Circumstances

These, I want to emphasise, are not really causes but are often linked with them as concomitants that influence the causal action.

Conditions make causality possible. Thus good health is the condition for hard labour. So, too, a closed window is the condition for opening it (if it is not closed, it cannot be opened: I can only open it on condition that it be closed). But we would hardly say that good health caused the work to be done much less that the closedness of the window caused it to open!

Occasions make the work of the cause easier. Thus, if the hinges are well oiled, my causality of opening the window is rendered easier. It would not be correct to say that the well oiled hinges opened the window.

Qualifying Circumstances as their name indicates, "stand around" (Latin, *circum* + *stare*) the cause as it works and thus, somehow or other, modify the cause at work. Sometimes these circumstances are morally relevant. To indulge in bribery or corruption reflects on the cause in a morally negative manner. However, if the agent or cause who does the bribery is a priest, this makes the agent more seriously guilty inasmuch as, being a priest, he is supposed to give moral leadership to the community. The fact that he is a priest does not add to his activity of bribing: it just makes the same act more heinous. At other times, circumstances may be morally neutral, such as whether it was noon or 2.00 p.m. when the deed was done or whether the agent was wearing black shoes or chappals at the time of action.

PART THREE

ON BE-ING OF BEINGS

Chapter 9

Be-ing (Existence)

Here we deal with the dynamic act of Be-ing, that is the verbal aspet of Be-ing. It is the possibility of beings and the foundation of beings. We explore the dynamic Be-ing which makes being possible!

a. Heidegger and Maréchal

In this chapter, we come to grips with the main work of metaphysics, according to Heidegger: the enquiry into the Being (act of existence) of beings (things that be). However, to a great extent, thanks to Maréchal, we have already done this. What occupies us mostly in this chapter, then, is to spell out and explicitate its implications.

But before we get down to that, it might be in order to quickly sum up and underline all that we have done in our analysis of intellectual dynamism, with particular relevance to our present interest. We note, first, first of all, that the critical enquiry into beings as well as into Being is discovered to be intertwined and inseparable. As Heidegger himself admits, we have no direct access to Being: we can only attain it in and through things which

> *"To be or not to be – that is the question!" (Shakespeare, Hamlet)*
> *"I am Who I am ..." (Exodus 3 : 14)*
> *"Let us be moral. Let us contemplate existence." (Mr. Pecksniff in Charles Dickens' Martin Chuzzlewit)*
> *"We will now discuss in a little more detail the struggle for existence....." (Charles Darwin, The Origin of Species)*
> *"Man's love is of man's life a thing apart, 'Tis a woman's whole existence." (Byron, Don Juan)*

we run into in our daily round, among which our own selves take the primacy. For, in making a critical enquiry into the act of existence as it is manifested in our own selves we already have an "insider's view", an intuition of what it is and involves. Our starting-point, the direct judgement, is a critical reflection on an undeniable activity of ours: hence, it lands us already in the existential order (i.e. Be-ing). Nor have we, like Descartes, imagined that we could elicit, as our most basic action, some inward-looking movement, divorced from all contact with the outside world. Indeed, there is no such thing: we can only know and affirm ourselves by knowing and affirming the external world in which we are. And such contact is grounded on their sensitive-rational act of direct judgement. Note, what is relevant for us is the affirmation that something exists: we may be mistaken in what concerns its essence (what it is), but that something does exist is undeniable. In other words, it is and has always been Being that we have been focusing on throughout the process, whether it be my existence, the existence of direct judgement or the existence of the affirmed object! Furthermore, the relentless analysis has shown that the ultimate goal of the existential act of direct judgement is yet another existence: pure, unlimited existence. Indeed, the only reason why "the things of this world" interest our intellectual activity at all is because they are partial realisations of that ultimate and unlimited existence which is responsible for our intellectual drive. We ended the quest by realising that we have to grant that this "unlimited existence" is not, cannot be, a mere mental fabrication (a concept) but something eminently real. Indeed, it is so real that all other realities derive their existence and actuality from it.

Let us now spell out some of the conclusions that can be derived from all this.

b. God, the unlimited existence

All things that be participate ontologically – that is, are totally and always dependent – on the unlimited existence. This, as we have seen, is nothing but creation seen from the point of view of the creative cause. Only God can create, for only uncreated, infinite, unlimited existence is God. In other words, God is existence, existence pure and simple, existence unrestrained by any composition or limitation (which comes to the same thing). In other words, the analysis of intellectual dynamism had revealed to us that the Being of beings is God! This doesn't mean that my existence is God: my existence is a finite, limited existence very specially participating in God: it is partially and secondarily what God is primarily and fully. Nor is the identification of God with unlimited existence anything startlingly new and unheard of. Thomas Aquinas did the same thing (by way of a questionable hermeneutics of Exodus 3:14). Thus, in ST Is, 13, 11, where he is discussing what is the most appropriate name for God, he concludes that "He who is" would be the best choice, even better than "The Good" for it does not signify any particular form. but rather existence itself. Since the existence of God is his essence and since this is true of nothing else. …, it is clear that this name is especially appropriate to God, for the meaning of a name is the form of the thing named.

Hence the most proper name of God is one which designates his basic dynamism (cf. the transcendentals). Just for the record, when God tells Moses, in response to the latter's demand to know God's name, "Jahweh", the meaning was not something like "I am the one whose very essence is to be", or "I am pure existence, the one that must be!" Situating Moses' question in the context of Jewish culture, it was more than likely that he was desirous of knowing God's name so as to be able – hopefully – to manipulate Him: after all, in Jewish culture, to know the name of someone/something meant to have some power over that being! So, as Jewish scholars tell us, God's answer most llikely meant something like, "I am who I am: it's none of your business!" A few others suggest that it might also imply, "I am the one who is true to his promises." Whatever be the merit of Aquinas' metaphysical comment in this connection, it can hardly be derived from an exegesis of the text.

c. The Be-ing of beings is personal

As we have seen, there is no real composition in Be-ing, in God. Above all, there is no materiality, the basic principle of indetermination which resists presence of self, as Rahner so rightly deduces.[1] Inasmuch as there is nothing in Be-ing to resist presence to self, Being is perfect self-transparency, perfect presence to self, perfect consciousness. But, as we have seen, an intellectual supposite is a person. Now the most perfect form of presence to self implies the most perfect form of knowing (or intellectuality, if you prefer). Thus God is personal. This, too, is nothing very revolutionary. Aristotle, approaching the issue from another path, concluded that God, by his very nature is *noesis noesos* (thought thinking of itself), again perfect self awareness.

However it is not at all difficult to show that Be-ing is also (and very specially), LOVE – which is the basis of the definition of person that I have championed, along with such giants like St. Albert the Great. For we have noted that all beings participate ontologically in Be-ing which, thereby, is their creator. As (unlimited) Be-ing, God has no need of anything. Hence God, in creating has nothing to gain: it is an act of pure giving, in which nothing is sought in return. This is nothing but another name for love, as per I John 4:8. The definition of God as Love is more revolutionary than we realise. Pascal culminated against "the God of philosophers" (like Aristotle) who is seen as a cold Absolute more or less wrapped up in himself (*noesis noeseos*). John's definition sees God as the very antithesis of a detached Absolute. Love is by

1 cf. His *Spirit in the World*.

Instead of starting with the heavens and firmament, mountains and oceans and drifting clouds, with things, and peeling all these away in a vain search for something, somehow more precious at their center, do the opposite. Instead of withdrawing inward, toward some imagined bit, some atom (which will surely slip away the moment you think you have it) – instead of this, try to proceed outward, and see heaven and earth, mountains and oceans and drifting clouds, all you have been taught to regard as things, as others, as foreign and distant, see all these as they are. You will be momentarily astonished to find yourself and nature in one and the same; and far from dreading nothingness, which now seems like sickness, and hardly worthy of anyone, which is how you began all this, your state of mind will be just the opposite. You will rejoice in being, in nature, in your self, which will now have ceased to be any mystery, and you will finally understand without seeking further what Spinoza meant by the intellectual love of God.[2]

its very nature relational. This necessary relational nature of God is seen in His/Her inner life whereby He/She is, in effect, a community (Trinity), not an isolated monad. This relationally spills over in the free act of creation which binds all creatures to Him/Her inextricably. He/She creates but does so out of no lack or need – purely out of the unconditional act of sharing love!

d. Be-ing is bliss

Be-ing is perfect self awareness and is devoid of any kind of limit whatsoever. Hence Be-ing is perfectly aware of its fullness, of the fact that there is nothing lacking. This, in turn, is but another word for BLISS, UNALLOYED JOY. Thus we can say, in agreement with the basic insight of Indian thought, that our enquiry into the Be-ing of beings (which gives us an insight into the Unlimited Be-ing in which they participate) is – as the ancient Indian sages had intuited – *sat-cit-Œnanda* (Being-consciousness-joy). Indeed, approaching reality from the more immanent perspective in keeping with our Indian tradition, one could make a case for these as the three basic transcendentals, corresponding to the one-true-good that swim into our ken when beings are viewed from the complementary Western whereby we go out of ourselves in a cognitive act of exteriorisation. Of course the "Indian transcendentals" would also be applied analogically to beings, inasmuch as they participate or share in it at various degrees – in what the ultimate Be-ing is fully.

It is no slight encouragement to us when we discover that traditional Eastern and Western metaphysics show little difference in their final conclusions ... just as there is scarce any major discrepancy to be found in the sharings of the great mystics of all religions. While speaking of Rudolf Otto in our *Rites and Rituals*[3] we indicated that there is practical unanimity that the core of the

2 Taylor, *Metaphysics*, 126.

3 Cyril Desbruslais, JDV, Pune.

encounter with the *ganz Andere* (the wholly other) is the experience of the *mysterium fascinans*: one realises that what one is faced with is something wholly other than anything one has experienced in this world (hence "mystery" is the best name for it); one's first reaction is awe and fear – one trembles as one suddenly becomes more and more aware of the all holiness of this other and of one's pervasive unworthiness: indeed, one's first reaction invariably is headlong flight; then comes a culminating, overwhelming conviction that the Other is gracious, grace-radiating and seems to be saying, "Come closer. Don't be afraid." Finally, the moment of loving mystical oneness (climaxing in adoration, prayer or worship) gives way to a prophetic sending forth to set others free. The grand finale of the meeting with God (or Be-ing) is the sense of commission, of being sent forth to do the work of justice. Of course, I have over-simplified and hurried things along a bit. It doesn't always unravel itself in such clear, chronological and pointed direction, but it can be discerned to be "at work" in that way nevertheless. Mystics and metaphysicians seem to meet each other at this climactic moment of union.

e. Responding to Be-ing

A concluding word about the reactions and responses that the encounter with Be-ing elicits from us. There seems to be, once again, a threefold dimension, interrelated and intertwined here too.

There is first (logically, not necessarily chronologically) a moment of enlightened encounter. As one personally meets Be-ing, one is gradually purified of wrong notions and attitudes as regards the Supreme Reality. This calls for a lot of openness and honesty as it often entails letting go of some of our favourite prejudices and brain-washed rigidities. Then – since the will follows the intellect – comes the moment of love. Corrected, purified knowledge of Be-ing, derived from an inter-personal encounter, calls forth from one a great surge of love – love for the gracious goodness of the Other. And as one is more and more caught up in the outgoing, unconditional love of Be-ing, one cannot but find oneself seized and carried along that same outgoing movement of sharing, of unconditional love to other beings. In other words, there comes the third and final movement of action, benevolent and beneficent action for those in need of it – action for justice.

And, once again, we find we join hands with the great mystics and sages of India. For what are these three moments but the traditional *margas* or paths to the Absolute: *jnana* (knowledge), *bhakti* (devotion or love) and *karma* (action or service). What may need to be emphasised here, however, is that there is to be no water-tight compartmentalising of the three, much less an endless debate as to which of the three, in isolation, is "the most excellent way". For knowledge cannot be liberative unless it be informed by love (else it could descend into proud Gnosticism) and love cannot be redemptive without being enlightened by knowledge (otherwise we would be led to all manner of fanaticism) and neither of the two are fully authentic until they spell themselves out in justice-seeking actions for all beings.

Finally we can find yet another assimilative echo of all these in the other well-known triad, faith-hope-love. Nor can these, in the last analysis, be separated from each other. Faith cannot be really salvific, if it is merely "belief that". It has to be "belief in" and we can only believe in one whom we love. Hope is nothing but loving, trust-filled action for justice, an action that never wanes in spite of difficulties and apparent failures because it is filled with hope that is grounded in faith and love. I leave it to the student to discover for her/himself how faith-hope-love, *jnana-bhakti-karma*, *mysterium-tremendum-fascinans*, *sat-cit-ananda*, one-true-good and Father-Son-Spirit are intimately bonded together. What God had joined together, let us not (by unwarranted metaphysical speculation) seek to put asunder.

"My end is my beginning!" (Mary, Queen of Scots)

EDITOR'S CONCLUSION

As we have seen, metaphysics is the branch of philosophy responsible for the study of existence. It is the foundation of a worldview. It answers the question "What is?" It encompasses everything that exists, as well as the nature of existence itself. It says whether the world is real, or merely an illusion. It is a fundamental view of the world around us.

It is important, since it is the foundation of philosophy. Without an explanation or an interpretation of the world around us, we would be helpless to deal with reality. We could not feed ourselves, or act to preserve our lives. The degree to which our metaphysical worldview is correct is the degree to which we are able to comprehend the world, and act accordingly. Without this firm foundation, all knowledge becomes suspect. Any flaw in our view of reality will make it more difficult to live, in spite of postmodern thinking.

In this sense, metaphysics provides us with a frame for our living, a norm for relating with the world and a basis for being who we are. Metaphysics thus gives us a perspective or framework, which can collectively shape the world we live in and the persons that we are! That is what Dr Cyril Desbruslais has inspired us to do through this book.

In this concluding session, we focus on the role of science in giving us a framework for our lives. We try to show that science today is trying to understand the whole as a whole – a metaphysical enterprise. If science takes this task seriously, we want to show, philosophy and religion also need to take the search for the ultimate meaning of our reality (including our lives, vision and experiences) earnestly!

a. Encounter Between Metaphysics and Science/Religion

The 20th century saw that philosophy and its life-long partner, metaphysics, have been divorced from many other disciplines of study, especially from science and humanities. The result has been an abandoning of the *big* questions and the emergence of the age of nihilism that had to be a necessary consequence of such a break. In fact, we could understand nihilism as a condition in which the *big questions* are not allowed to be asked.[1] What we gain from this separation is a certain liberation from theological (or religious) speculations. At the same time we also lose a serious and overarching vision of existence and our direction forward. In short, we lose our meaningfulness in the deep sense. We forget the larger direction of our lives. We do not have any strong footing on a larger story within which we can make sense of our limited experiences.

"Vanity of vanities" was the great nihilistic assertion. This led to the elimination of religion from both public and private spheres. This was due to the influence of positivism in science and postmodernism in philosophy.[2]

Nevertheless, "metaphysical thinking hasn't ceased, in fact it's healthier than ever in what are the most unlikely places: in the halls of science," claims Paul Adkin.[3] It is the scientists of today – the quantum physicists and cosmologists – who are now asking the big questions of life and speculating on the origin of things and all the multiplicity that has grown from that origin like never before.[4] They want to know the direction and goal of the universe both from a physical and metaphysical perspectives.

Thus the contemporary scientific community is obsessed with the big questions: What are we?; Who are we really? Where have we come from? Where are we going? In fact, ideas of *fine tuning* in the universe, or multiverse theories, leave fertile ground for religious thought and metaphysical speculations. For instance, the idea of multiverse implies that if there have been endless amounts of universes, eventually one of them will have to work. In an infinity, our existence is a mathematically certainty.

But this reduction, or expansion, of our necessary reality created by the mathematical necessities of infinity doesn't have to diminish the meaningfulness of our existence. Even if purpose is accidentally formed, when we know what it is, "we must not only acknowledge it, but embrace it and

---

1 The Big Questions are necessarily scientific and philosophical questions that affect our larger human concerns. They may be philosophical and metaphysical. They are indicated in the debates opened up by John Templeton Foundation's initiatives. See https://www.speechanddebate.org/big-questions/.

2 For this section I am indebted to Paul Adkin's excellent article, "The Importance of Metaphysics," I21/04/2013) which deals with metaphysics from the perspective of physics or cosmology. https://pauladkin.wordpress.com/2013/04/21/the-importance-of-metaphysics. In this section I deal exclusively with the positivistic (or scientific) treatment, since the postmodern approach is taken up in the next book of the Series written by Desbruslais.

3 Adkin 2013.

4 An example of this can be seen in this TED talk by Brian Greene. See his "Is our universe the only universe?" February 2012. https://www.ted.com/talks/brian_greene _why_is_our_ universe_fine_tuned_for_life? language=en. For more related talks see http://philosophy-of-cosmology.ox.ac.uk/tag/ted-talks/

rejoice in it."[5] The real purpose of human beings and of the universe, it may be noted, may lie in something very simple. Philosophers have been pondering over these questions and attempting to find answers.[6]

In this way, it seems that metaphysics is a stronger element than 20th century philosophy, giving a new metaphysical and teleological theories derived from quantum and cosmological discoveries of today. This metaphysical renaissance of meaning to be provided into the fabric of science can bring about a return to the idea of philosophy or metaphysics in its purest form. This takes us to the pre-Socratic purity of the big questions, to borrow the Heideggerian understanding.

b. Moving Beyond Kant

Immanuel Kant, the father of critical philosophy, considered metaphysics, as expressed in his *Critique of Pure Reason*, as necessary but mostly useless. So he writes in the penultimate chapter of the second edition his Critique: "*Metaphysic is divided into that of the speculative and that of the practical use of pure reason, and is, accordingly, either the metaphysic of nature, or the metaphysic of ethics. The former contains all the pure rational principles—based upon conceptions alone (and thus excluding mathematics)—of all theoretical cognition; the latter, the principles which determine and necessitate a priori all action.*"

The metaphysics of nature is investigated in the sciences, especially in cosmology and quantum physics. The discoveries made recently by contemporary cosmology leads to deeper questions – philosophical investigation and metaphysical queries, leading to what the end-goals of cosmos and humanity could be! Such an investigation also explores the possible goal of the universe and that of human beings too! It tries to answer the question: What is reality? Where does it go to? Who are human beings? What is the destiny of the humans?

Kant believed that it was pointless to think seriously about concepts beyond the *a priori* realities of time and space. Contemporary cosmological calculations and quantum physics have pushed our thinking light-years away from the universe that could be conceived in Kant's time. Surely, we have moved way beyond Kant's understanding both in cosmology and metaphysics.

We now know enough about our universe to look for answers into the great mystery of how the universe works within the existence of possible multiverses, "dark matter," black holes and vacuum fluctuations. We can look at the world we are able to explore and wonder at our own limited but

5 Adkin 2013.

6 Adkin 2013. One useful site which attempts to foster a world-view (or metaphysics) in consonance with contemporary scientific findings is by Richard Golden, http://sciphilos.info/.

incredible possibilities. We can ask ourselves what really hold the cosmos together. "Cosmologists can now express valid suspicious that the Big Bang doesn't, because it cannot, explain the entire composition and fine-tuned functioning of the universe as we know it today. At the cosmological and the quantum level, everything is much greater and more beautiful and mysterious than it ever was before, and understanding that mystery and beauty is our own mysteriously beautiful purpose for 'being' in this magic place."[7]

c. Search for a Theory of Everything

At the scientific level today, this search for meaning and significance has also been pursued at a different level. Specially in the last century many scientists have been trying to trace a theory of everything. [8] It is said that Albert Einstein spent his last few hours on Earth scribbling something on a piece of paper in a last attempt to formulate a theory of everything. After about 60 years, another legendary figure in theoretical physics, Stephen Hawking, may have left us with similar thoughts. Using the "M-theory," he too had been trying to find a complete theory of the universe!

Like Hawking, since the formulation of Einstein's theory of general relativity in 1915, every theoretical physicist has been dreaming of reconciling our understanding of the infinitely small world of atoms and particles with that of the infinitely large scale of the cosmos. While the latter is effectively described by Einstein's equations, the former is predicted with extraordinary accuracy by the so-called Standard Model of fundamental interactions.

Our current understanding is that the interaction between physical objects is described by four fundamental forces. Two of them – gravity and electromagnetism – are relevant for us on a macroscopic level, we deal with them in our everyday life. The other two, called strong and weak interactions, act on a very small scale and become relevant only when dealing with subatomic processes.

The great physicists and cosmologists are driven by a passion to find that beautiful, simple description of the world that can explain everything. And

---

7 Adkin 2013.

8 The recent film "The Theory of Everything" tells the story of Stephen Hawking, who managed to become a world-famous physicist despite being confined to a wheelchair by a degenerative disease. It is, in fact, mostly about his relationship with his ex-wife Jane, but it does find a bit of time to explain the theory of everything that Hawking has spent his career searching.Hawking, of happy memory, certainly didn't lack ambition. Hawking has been one of many physicists trying to come up with a "theory of everything", a single theory that will explain everything about our universe. He was following in the footsteps of Albert Einstein, who tried and failed to devise such a theory.

although we are not quite there yet, we wouldn't have a chance without the sharp, creative minds of people like Einstein and Hawking.[9]

Finding a theory of everything would be a remarkable achievement, enabling us making sense of all the weird and wonderful things in our universe. For decades, confident physicists have said that one is just around the corner. But at the scientific realm, we are still waiting for a total understanding and complete explanation of it.

d. Finally ...

Similar to the scientific quest to understand the world holistically, as philosophers and human beings, we need to take stoke of the world metaphysically. We need to recognise that scientific facts and theories must be taken seriously when we formulate our metaphysical views. At the same time, we cannot leave the metaphysical search only to the scientific community.

Drawing from science and other resources, we need to make sense of reality and our life therein. We need to have a conceptual and metaphysical framework, which does justice to the modern world! Such a conceptual framework, philosophical outlook or metaphysical world-view can shape our lives and that of the world!

Thus, through metaphysics, we can approach reality and be fascinated by it. We can pose questions and live into the answers. We can make better sense of the nature of the cosmos and ourselves. We can delve deep into the mysterious world – both the inner world of our consciousness and the outer world of reality – and be enamoured by it!

9 Lorenzo Bianchi "Was This Stephen Hawking's Theory of Everything?" *News Week,* 19.3.18 at *https://www.newsweek.com/stephen-hawking-general-relativity-quantum-mechanics-m-theory-850581*

APPENDIX

I. An Indian Approach to Metaphysics

In this appendix, after having elaborated on Metaphysics from a predominantly Western perspective, we try to outline very briefly the approach of Indian philosophy contrasted with that of Western philosophy. [1] We also see some of its predominant characteristics. We finally attempt at focusing on some convergences between the two traditions. Here our treatment will be seminal and partial.

a. An Indian approach

Unlike the western philosophical approach, the Indian approach does not attempt to analyse objects or find a system or framework to give order and meaning to the external world. It is primarily concerned with the basic problem of one's suffering or bondage, which is the experience of pain and pleasure and of the world. So, the aim of the general Indian philosophy is to seek *moksa* or release from the world of changes and *maya*. In this quest for salvation the Indian metaphysics has concentrated on conscious experience, the "I-hood", since in all the changing vicissitudes of life only the sense of "I" remains unchanged.

While looking into my own self and examining my sense of "I" it is not possible to discover a beginning or an end to this sense of "I". I cannot imagine a time when "I" was not, nor picture to myself a condition when "I" shall not be. I cannot find limitations in myself. But while looking outside of myself into the objective experiences that I am confronted with, I gather the sense of instability, flux and limitations. Thus, Indian metaphysics seeks for an ideal reality to aim at, which is the model for permanence and stability. If we keep this aim in mind, it is not surprising that the Indian tradition has chosen the

---

1 This is a modified summary by the editor of J.B. Chethimattam, *Consciousness and Reality: An Indian Approach to Metaphysics*, Bangalore, 1967, pp. 1-14 & 241-249.

conscious Ego inside rather than the objective reality outside to be its primary focus.

From the very beginning of philosophical thinking India had concentrated on life and vital evolution as the model of its conception of reality. The cosmological myths which conceived the origin of the world in terms of biological generation found its articulation in Indian philosophy too. Accordingly, the universe is said to have evolved from the primeval golden seed (egg), *Hiranyagarbha*. The origin of the universe could be traced to the cosmic egg which splits into two forming heaven and earth.[2]

In Purushasukta the evolution of the cosmos is derived from Purusha, the Supreme Person:

> A thousand heads hath Purusha, a thousand eyes, a thousand feet. On every side pervading earth he fills a space ten fringes wide. This Purusha is all that yet hath been and all that is to be ... All creatures are one-fourth of him, three-fourths eternal life in heaven.[3]

It is further interesting to note that with the development of thinking the notion of development of Being, *sat*, the participle of the verb *asti*, "to be" is introduced. "*Asti*" in Sanskrit is much more significant than the corresponding "*esti*" of Greek. *Asti* is not just limited to the function of a copula, but has an existential connotation to *sat* and so has a strong existential meaning.

The state before the emergence of *sat* is named as *asat* or non-being. Further *sat* is said to emerge from the womb of *asat*, in which was the embryonic water as yet "unaccented", i.e. without the aid of any other principle, but solely by the orgasmic heat of procreative impulse or *kama*: "Thereafter arose desire in the beginning, desire, the primal seed and germ of spirit." This thought finds its echo in other Upanishadic writings:[4]

> In the beginning this was non-existent. From it was born what exists. That made itself its Self, therefore it is called self-made.
>
> In the beginning there was nothing here whatsoever. By Death indeed all this was concealed, – by hunger; for death is hunger. Death thought, "Let me have a body."

b. Primacy of Being over Non-Being

Our beginning from *asat* leads us to realise and affirm the primacy of Being. Being is the beginning and origin of the whole reality. This is clear from the instruction of Uddalaka to his son found in Chadogya Upanisad:[5]

2 Cf. Chethimattam, 7.

3 Rg Veda, X, 90.

4 Rg Veda, X, 90.

5 Chandogya Upanisha, VI, I, 4-6; VI, ii, 1-2.

> My boy, just as through a clod of clay, all that is made of clay would become known; all products being due to words, a mere name; the clay alone is real.
>
> My boy, just as through a single ingot of gold, all that is made of god would be known…
>
> Just as through a single nail clipper, all that is made of iron would become known …
>
> In the beginning, my dear, this was Being only, – one, without a second. – Some say that, in the beginning, this was non-being, only one, without a second. From that non-being sprang Being. But how could it be so, my dear? – said he: How could Being be born from non-being? In fact, this was Being only, in the beginning, one, without a second.
>
> All these creatures, my dear, have their root in Being, reside in Being and rest in Being … Now that which is this subtle reality, in that has all this its Self; that is the Truth; that thou art, O Svetaketu.

This key affirmation of the primacy of Being over Non-Being becomes such a central principle of Indian metaphysics that almost every Indian metaphysician was obliged to give a commentary on this text.

The difference in outlook between the Indian and Western view is evident. It may be assumed that Parmenides is seeking the real object of thought and speech. Uddalaka is inquiring into "that by which the unrevealed is revealed, the non-understood understood, and the unknown known," that is, the ultimate basis of all reality that remains hidden from ordinary experience. This *sat* is said to be unique, the source and origin of the whole reality.

In the same way in the Brihadaranyaka Upanishad Maitreyi, who cares only for immortality and not for worldly things is advised by Yajnavalkya, her ascetic husband that the knowledge of the Self, of *atman* alone leads to immortality: "The self is to be seen, to be heard, to be perceived, to be marked, and everything else only for the sake of the self."[6]

This *atman* is in everything just as the sound in the individual notes of music or salt in water. According to one line of thought in Brihadaranyaka Upanishad being and non-being, material and immaterial, mortal and immortal, solid and fluid and other opposites are two forms of Brahman, the Supreme Reality. The two together make the world of our experience. Extending this thought further we can say that *sat* (=being) together with *tyat* (=indefinite) makes *satyam* (=true). But Brahman who is beyond all these opposites can be only indicated by "not this," "not this" (*neti, neti*) designations in terms of our experience; for He is *satyasya satyam*, the truth of the true.[7]

6 Brihadaranyaka Upanishad. II, iv, 1-8.

7 Cf. Chettimattam, 10.

Further in Kathopanishad the pious Brahman boy Naciketas is sent by his angry father to the god of death, Yama. On arrival at the palace of god Naciketa receives a bad welcome because Death was not present. Later when Yama came to know about the dishonour done to the Brahman boy, he grants Naciketas three boons, which Naciketas could freely wish. Naciketa asks for the knowledge about the Ultimate Reality. After having ascertained the sincerity of Naciketa's wish Death explains to Naciketas that the Nature of the Real as symbolised by the mystic "OM" is Brahman. Brahman is:[8]

The self, smaller than small, greater than the great,
Is the Atman that is set in the heart of a creature here …
Sitting, he proceeds afar:
Lying he goes everywhere …
Him who is the bodiless among bodies,
Stable among the unstable,
The great, all-pervading Atman,
On recognising Him, the wise man sorrows not.

Here it is very significant that the doctrine of the Ultimate Reality is given by Death. Death is the great teacher about Reality. On hearing this teaching by Death, Nacikatas becomes freed from all worldly attachment and attains Brahman.

c. The method

The realisation of the Ultimate reality is not accessible by the sense organs nor by reasoning. Ultimate Reality lies beyond sense experience and the generalisations or deductive or inductive inferences. So the procedure of Upanishads to attain this Ultimate Reality is directed to the interior of the self.

So in Brihadaranyaka Upanishad Yanavalkya shows how one can proceed from the crude material earth, through the elements of water, air and fire in the increasing order of subtlety to the general notion of being: "He who dwells in all beings, and within all beings, whom all beings do not know, whose body all being are, and who rules all beings from within, he is the Self, the ruler within, the immortal."[9]

Beyond the general aspects of material beings (*adhibhuta*) are the various levels of consciousness: one has to go through the layers of life, speech, the senses of hearing, seeing to reach the internal sense of mind and knowledge and further proceed to the inner core of our conscious self which is the pure aspect of witness. This witness leads to realise the Ultimate Reality as pure witness, i.e. as *Sakti*.

8 Katha Upanishad, I, ii, 16-22.

9 Brihadaranyaka Upanishad, III, vii, 15; III, viii, 7, 13-22.

"He is thy Self, the ruler within, the immortal; unseen, but seeing; unheard, but hearing; unperceived, but perceiving; unknown but knowing. There is no other seer but he … there is no other knower but he. This is thy Self, the ruler within, I immortal."[10] This leads the search for the ultimate reality to the pure conscious Self, which is the purest and subtlest core of all things.

Similar method of procedure appears in other Upanishads too. Kena Upanishad asks the basic question at the very beginning itself: "Impelled by whom, at whose will does the mind move, does the vital airs act, by whose movement does the speech speak, the eye and the ear and their presiding deities attain their objects?"[11] The answer evidently is "the ear of the ear, the mind of the mind, the speech of speech and the eye of the eye"[12] which is the Real beyond and is indicated by "*Tadvanam*," the goal and object of all aspirations. Thus, the Ultimate Reality is so subtle that none of the human faculties can grasp Him. But one has to go through (beyond) the human faculties to reach Him.

This interior search is further evidenced by a parable from Kena Upanishad.[13] Once the gods had gathered together and boasting of their feats in defeating the demons. Suddenly an unknown deity appears near them. The God Agni, fire is deputed to find out who the intruder is. As a condition for answering his question the unknown god challenges Agni to burn a straw put forth by him. Agni tries, fails and so turns back. Then the god of Air, Vayu is also sent back since he could not even blow the straw of the stranger god. When Indra, the god of the sky, approaches the stranger the Deity vanishes suddenly. Finally, Uma, the goddess of divine wisdom appears to them in mid-air and informs them that the strange Deity was Brahman, the Supreme and it is only through Him that they defeated the Demons. Thus, actions represented by sense experiences represented by fire and air cannot lead one to Ultimate Reality. Even the intellect (represented by Indra, the god of the sky) cannot directly attain Reality, which can be grasped only by divine wisdom in mid-air, that is, in the cave of the heart, by a sort of intuition.

So the method to attain the Ultimate Reality is to go beyond the sense to the ultimate immutable reality, that is, the basis of all intelligibility and consciousness.

d. The convergence

As we know, the great figures of Indian philosophy, Sankara and Ramanuja start from consciousness (while Sankara stresses abstract and distinctless

10 Brihadaranyaka Upanishad, III, vii, 23.

11 Cf. Chethimattam, 12.

12 Kena Upanishad, II & III.

13 Kena Upanishad, II, 3.

notion of consciousness; Ramanuja concentrates on self-consciousness), seek an integral vision of reality, and strive to interpret the world of finite beings in relation with the Absolute Consciousness, Brahman. Such an attempt is incomparable to the Western tradition, even if we take Thomas Aquinas. Thus the differences with Western traditions are clear. In spite of them, there are points of convergence and complementarity as pointed out by Chethimattam.[14]

1. Western metaphysical tradition proceeds towards reality primarily by a rational analysis of thought, implying that the laws of thought reveal the laws of reality. The Indian approach, on the other hand, takes our conscious self-awareness as the authentic reality and tries to discover its immutable ground and authentic condition in the plurality of every day experience.
2. The Western tradition beginning with the analysis of reality takes plurality as a fact and tries to solve the problem of unity in terms of metaphysical categories like analogy of being. In contrast, making consciousness as the starting point, the Indian tradition takes the absolute unity of all things in Supreme Consciousness as a fact, and proceeds to resolve the problem of multiplicity not through exact definitions and categories but pointing to the ineffable mystery of reality.
3. The rational metaphysical tradition tries to solve the anomaly of finite being by bringing in the principle of causality. The formal cause predominates and even the efficient cause acts in virtue of the form immanent in it. For Indian philosophy, causality which explains the relevance of finite beings is of secondary importance. It gives importance to material cause as the ultimate ground and material principle of all things operative and the formal cause is reduced to the instrumental functions and define reality from outside.
4. The act of personal encounter is a converging factor in both the traditions. The basic freedom and responsibility of the conscious finite self is accepted in both traditions. Every finite being finds meaning only in the context of his communion or encounter with other persons and finally with the Supreme Person.

It is evident that Western and Indian traditions diverge to a large extent. In the divergence of approaches the final question, according to Chethimattam[15] is not one of truth and error or right and wrong. What is of significance is to recognise that the two approaches are complementary and not contradictory. Only a misunderstanding of the approaches can give way

14 Cf. Chethimattam, 241-243.

15 Cf. Chethimattam, 248-249.

to total incomprehension and misunderstanding. It might also be admitted that both the approaches have its strengths and shortcomings. The clarity of concepts and accurate understanding of rational approach should not assume that it has understood the reality in itself. Consciousness on the other hand tries to present reality in one's own self, within reach of immediate understanding and it tends to forget distinctions and smoothens out the limits which define the finite in contrast to the Infinite. Though we may not be able to fuse both the approaches into one, we need both the approaches. We can maintain their proper character, and encourage and promote the dialogue that emerges from these two horizons. That will benefit both the horizons and to those living within these horizons.

II. Some Questions for Reflection

1. How do you show that metaphysics is the basis of philosophy?
2. How do you "define" metaphysics? What are the difficulties with "defining" it?
3. What is the starting point of metaphysics, according to Marechal?
4. Who are some of the other neo-Thomist philosophers of the last century?
5. Briefly explain the transcendental analysis of Marechal.
6. How do you that direct judgement is a metaphysical fact.
7. How do you show that the Unlimited Existence really exist? (elaborate any <u>one</u> of the three "proofs" given).
8. How do you show that starting from direct judgement, we experience a limit, which opens us to a limitless being?
9. How can you prove that Unlimited Essence cannot exist?
10. Can we prove that the world is really real? Why?
11. "All limited beings depend totally on the unlimited being." Please demonstrate this.
12. "Human beings are openness to the Unlimited Existence." Demonstrate this statement.
13. What are transcendentals?
14. What is "beauty"? What is its significance as a transcendental?
15. Take any one of the transcendentals and show the significance of the particular transcendental and its relevance for our life.
16. What is change? How do you explain change in terms of act and potency?
17. What is matter and form? How do you differentiate one from the other.
18. How do you distinguish essence from existence?
19. What is the principle of causality?
20. What is the difference between intrinsic and extrinsic causality?
21. What are the varieties of final (or efficient) cause?
22. What are Hume's objections to causality?
23. Who is a "person" metaphysically?
24. How do you show that persons are "ends in themselves"?
25. What is Parmenides' position on change?
26. How do you show that change is not substitution?
27. Is there anything that must be true of absolutely everything that exists?
28. Must anything that exists have intrinsic properties?
29. What are properties? Are they universals, or tropes, or . . .?
30. Must anything that exists stand in some relation to something else?
31. Must anything that exists be completely determinate, or can there be vague objects?
32. Can there be things that exist that are not in time?
33. Is there anything that is not part of the spatiotemporal world?

34. What are the truthmakers for mathematical statements?
35. What are numbers?
36. Can there be necessarily existent entities?
37. What is it for something to be an actual entity?
38. Is everything that exists an actual entity?
39. What are the truthmakers for statements of logical possibility?
40. Do merely possible worlds exist?
41. What sorts of things are possible worlds?
42. Is change really possible?
43. Can there be things that are in principle unobservable?
44. Can one make sense of a non-reductionist view of theoretical entities?
45. Can there be aspects of reality that are in principle unknowable?
46. Why is there something, rather than nothing?
47. Could the world contain only dispositional properties?
48. Can there be pure dispositional properties – that is, properties that have no categorical basis?
49. What is time?
50. Is time real, or an illusion?
51. Could time be cyclic?
51. Can there be time without change?
53. Is space real, or an illusion?
54. Is space itself an entity, or is it reducible to spatial relations between objects and events?
55. What are laws of nature?
56. Do laws of nature govern the occurrence of events in time?
57. Are there laws of nature?
58. What is causation?
59. Is causation real, or an illusion?
60. Could a cause succeed its effect?
61. Could a cause and its effect be simultaneous?
62. Are causal facts supervenient upon non-causal facts?
63. Do causal relations between events presuppose causal laws?
64. Is the world a deterministic one?
65. What are persisting substances? Are they bundles of properties, or properties plus a substratum, or . . . ?
66. What constitutes "identity over time"?
67. Do objects perdure, or endure?
68. Does the physical universe depend upon the existence of an immaterial creator?
69. Is there a necessarily existent being upon which the contingent world depends for its existence?
70. Could there be a person who was not in time?

71. Can persons be analyzed in terms of person-stages?
72. Is the self a bundle of experiences?
73. Is the self a bundle of powers?
74. Do humans involve immaterial souls?
75. Do humans involve any properties that are not reducible to the properties that characterize the inanimate world?
76. What is consciousness?
77. What is intentionality? What is it for a mental state to be 'about' something?
78. Could consciousness be a purely physical phenomenon?
79. Could intentionality be a purely physical phenomenon?
80. Are humans free?
81. Is freedom compatible with determinism?
82. Do humans possess libertarian free will?
83. Is there such a thing as agent-causation?

SELECT BIBLIOGRAPHY

Aquinas, Thomas and Jean T. Oesterle. *The Collected Works of St. Thomas Aquinas. The Disputed Questions on Truth: Volumes 1-3*. Charlottesville, Va: InteLex Corporation, 1993.

Aristotle, and C. D. C. Reeve. *Metaphysics*. Indianapolis; Cambridge : Hackett Publishing Company, 2016.

Aristotle, Philip H. Wicksteed, and Francis M. Cornford. *The Physics: Books I-Iv*. Cambridge, MA: Harvard University Press, 1957.

Augustine, and Edward Bouverie Pulsey. *The Confessions of S. Augustine*. Rockville, MD: Arc Manor, 2008.

Ayer, A.J. *Language, Truth and Logic*, London, V. Gollancz, 1951, 45.

Brown, Herold. "Causality and the Cosmos", in *Causality*, edited by George P. Adams et al., Berkeley, Univ. of California Press, 1932.

Carnap, Rudolf. *Philosophy and Logical Syntax*. London, Trench and Trubner and Co., 1935.

Chethimattam, John B.*Consciousness and Reality* Bangalore, Dharmaram College, 1967.

Coreth, Emerich and J. F. Donceel. *Metaphysics. English Ed. by Joseph Donceel; With a Critique by Bernard J.F. Lonergan*. [New York]: Herder and Herder, 1968.

Coreth, Emerich. *Grundriss der Metaphysik*, Tyrolia, Innsbruck, 1994.

Coreth, Emerich. *Metaphysik,* Tyrolia, Innsbruck, 1961.

Desbruslais, C. *Rites and Rituals*, (mimeographed notes), JDV, Pune, 1986.

Desbruslais, C. *History of Western Philosophy*, JDV, Pune, 1984.

Desbruslais, C. *Philosophy of the HumanPerson*, JDV, Pune, 1997.

Donceel, Joseph (ed) *Metaphysics* Herder and Herder, 1968.

Hagspiel, B. *Smiles and Chuckles*, Illinois, Mission Press, 1952.

Hume, David. *Treatise of Human Nature*. Place of publication not identified: Alpha Editions, 2017

Kant, Immanuel. *Critique of Pure Reason*. South Bend: Infomotions, Inc., 2000.

Loewenberg, J. "The Elasticity of the Idea of Causality," *Causality*, edited by Adams.

Maréchal, Joseph. *Cahiers* [especially the lastentitled *Le point de départde la métaphysique*] Paris, Desclée, 1949.

Marechal, Joseph. *Le point de départ de la métaphysique leçons sur le développement historique et théorique du problème de la connaissance*. Bruxelles: Ed. Universelle, 1944.

Mencken, H.L. *Minority Report*, New York, Alfred K. Knopf, 1956.

Pandikattu, Kuruvilla. *It's Time!*, JDV, Pune, 1997.

Pandikattu, Kuruvilla. *This Too Will Pass Away!: The Scientific Explanation and Religious Experience of Time Based on Michael Ende's Momo*. Pune: Jnanam, 2003.

Russell, B. *An Outline of Philosophy*, London, Allen & Unwin, 1927.

Shine, Daniel. *An Interior Metaphysics*. Massachusetts, Weston College, 1966.

Sweeney, Leo. *A Metaphysics of Authentic Existentialism*, New Jersey, Prentice-Hall, 1965.

Taylor, Richard. *Metaphysics*, Prentice-Hall, Inc, New Jersey, 1974, 8-9.

Thomas, Richard F. *Virgil, Georgics: 1*. Cambridge: Cambridge Univ. Press, 1988.

Wild, John "Realistic Defence of Causal Efficacy", in *Review of Metaphysics*, 2, June 1949.

Wilde, Oscar. *Lady Windermere's Fan: A Play About a Good Woman*. Newburyport: Open Road Media, 2018.

Wittgenstein, Ludwig. *Tractatus Logico-Philosophicus* Tran. & ed. D.F. Pears and B.F. McGuiness, London, Routledge and Kegan Paul, 1961. (First published in 1921.)

GLOSSARY

Accidents: See Essence.

Act: In its most general sense, act means a perfection and potency means a capacity or readiness for a perfection. Potency, in turn may be of two kinds, passive and active. A passive potency is the capacity to receive a certain perfection: for example, a man has the capacity to acquire fatness ... An active potency is the capacity to do particular perfective action. The faculty of sight, for instance, has the active potency to perceive colour – but not sound. A human being has the passive potency to acquire philosophical knowledge. But this is only because there is in him/her some active inner disposition for it which a chair say, has not! The problem of the reality of change is well accounted for using Aristotle's theory of act and potency.

Aseity (From Latin a "from" and se "self", plus -ity) is the property by which a being exists in and of itself, from itself, or exists as so-and-such of and from itself.

Avidya: delusion or ignorance. Its literal meaning is ignorance, misconceptions, misunderstandings, incorrect knowledge, and it is the opposite of Vidya. In Advaita Vedanta, the effect of avidya is to suppress the real nature of things and present something else in its place. ... Avidya relates to the individual Self (Ātman), while Maya is an adjunct of the cosmic Self (Brahman)

Causality: In his philosophical writings, Aristotle used the Greek word αἴτιον, aition, a neuter singular form of an adjective. The Greek word had meant, perhaps originally in a "legal" context, what or who is "responsible", mostly but not always in a bad sense of "guilt" or "blame"; alternatively it could mean "to the credit of" someone or something. The appropriation of this word by Aristotle and other philosophers reflects how the Greek experience of legal practice influenced the concern in Greek thought to determine what is responsible. The word developed other meanings, including its use in philosophy in a more abstract sense. About a century before Aristotle, the anonymous author of the Hippocratic text On Ancient Medicine had described the essential characteristics of a cause: "We must, therefore, consider the causes of each [medical] condition to be those things which are such that, when they are present, the condition necessarily occurs, but when they change to another combination, it ceases." In the present context, Aristotle used the four causes to provide different answers to the question, "because of what?" The four answers to this question illuminate different aspects of how a thing comes into being or of how an event takes place. Aristotle held that there were four kinds of answers to "why" questions (in Physics II, 3, and Metaphysics V, 2):

Matter: a change or movement's material cause, is the aspect of the change or movement which is determined by the material that composes the moving or changing things. For a table, that might be wood; for a statue, that might be bronze or marble.

Form: a change or movement's formal cause, is a change or movement caused by the arrangement, shape or appearance of the thing changing or moving. Aristotle says for example that the ratio 2:1, and number in general, is the cause of the octave.

Agent: a change or movement's efficient or moving cause, consists of things apart from the thing being changed or moved, which interact so as to be an agency of the change or movement. For example, the efficient cause of a table is a carpenter, or a person working as one, and according to Aristotle the efficient cause of a boy is a father.

End or purpose: a change or movement's final cause, is that for the sake of which a thing is what it is. For a seed, it might be an adult plant. For a sailboat, it might be sailing. For a ball at the top of a ramp, it might be coming to rest at the bottom.

The four "causes" are not mutually exclusive. For Aristotle, several answers to the question "why" have to be given to explain a phenomenon and especially the actual configuration of an object. For example, if asking why a table is such and such, a complete explanation, taking into account the four causes, would sound like this: This table is solid and brown because it is made of wood (matter), it does not collapse because it has four legs of equal length (form), it is as such because a carpenter made it starting from a tree (agent), it has these dimensions because it is to be used by men and women (end).

Change: The process of causing a function, practice, or thing to become different somehow compared to what it is at present or what it was in the past. There is some element of continuity in change. So there is no a total or radical break with the past. In Thomistic metaphysics we explain it in terms of act and potency.

Cogito: the principle establishing the existence of a being from the fact of its thinking or awareness, popularised by Descartes. *Cogito*, ergo sum, (Latin: "I think, therefore I am) dictum coined by the French philosopher René Descartes in his *Discourse on Method* (1637). This was the end of the search Descartes conducted for a statement that could not be doubted. He found that he could not doubt that he himself existed, as he was the one doing the doubting in the first place.

Direct judgement: An undeniable fact of our life, Direct Judgement is a simple statement affirming (or denying) something. E.g.: The cat is on the mat. Or The cat is a pet animal. Here we necessarily affirm, through it, that a being exists and what it is – these are the elements of existence and essence, respectively.

End-in-itself: A human being is end-in-itself. Here end is opposed to means or "means to an end". The philosopher Immanuel Kant said that rational human beings should be treated as an end in themselves and not as a means to something else. The fact that we are human has value in itself. This is his articulation of the categorical imperative.

Essence: essence or "whatness" (Latin, *quidditas*) of a thing (being) comprises two dimensions: that which gives primary or basic determination (=substance) and that which provides further or secondary determination (=accidents). Substance designates what a thing is basically. Accidents tell us what concrete qualities this particular instance of that substance carries along with it. Thus a being is basically a horse or a cat or a human being and secondarily a black horse, a fat cat or a tall human being. Here, horse, cat and human being are substances, while black, fat and tall are accidents.

Existence is the "thatness" of a being. It points to the fact of a thing existing. Usually it contrasted to the "whatness" (qualities, attributes, etc) of a thing, known as Essence.

Extrinsic causes on the other hand, are and remain – completely distinct (separate) from the effect. Thus we have the *efficient cause*, which "makes the effect come into existence either totally or partially". God is the efficient cause of the world and the carpenter is the efficient cause of the table.

Final cause: See Finality, principle of.

Finality, principle of: The principle of finality is in a sense the most fundamental of them, given that the final cause is 'the cause of causes': for, again in Aquinas's' view an efficient cause can bring an effect in to being only if it is 'directed towards' that effect; and it is ultimately in that sense that the effect is 'contained in' the efficient cause. Aristotle defines the end, purpose, or final "cause" (*telos*) as that for the sake of which a thing is done.

Form: See Matter.

Gnosticism: a prominent heretical movement of the 2nd-century Christian Church, partly of pre-Christian origin. Gnostic doctrine taught that the world was created and ruled by a lesser divinity, the demiurge, and that Christ was an emissary of the remote supreme divine being, esoteric knowledge (gnosis) of whom enabled the redemption of the human spirit. It holds that humans are divine souls trapped in the ordinary physical (or material) world. They say that the world was made by an imperfect spirit. The imperfect spirit is thought to be the same as the God of Abraham. Some Gnostic groups saw Jesus as sent by the supreme being, to bring gnosis to the Earth.

Intellectual dynamism: Joseph Maréchal' method of transcendental analysis of direct judgement based on "intellectual dynamism." It looks into the conditions that make intellectual dynamism possible. Applying this analysis on direct judgement, he comes up with essence (necessarily limited) and existence (limited, but not necessarily). This is the method of his metaphysics that leads to Unlimited Existence.

Intrinsic causes: These causes comprise those which are part of the effect hence the name 'intrinsic'. There are two such causes: (a) the *formal cause*, which specifies the effect. Thus, the human and canine "souls" are the formal cause of a human being and a dog, respectively; (b) the *material cause*: that out of which the effect is made. Thus, wood is the material cause of the table and various pieces of metal and glass, fitted together, are the material cause of my spectacles.

Manicheanism: a dualistic religious system with Christian, Gnostic, and pagan elements, founded in Persia in the 3rd century by Manes (*c.* 216– *c.* 276) and based on a supposed primeval conflict between light and darkness. It was widespread in the Roman Empire and in Asia, and survived in eastern Turkestan (Xinjiang) until the 13th century. Founded by the Iranian prophet Mani, Manichaeism taught an elaborate dualistic cosmology describing the struggle between a good, spiritual world of light, and an evil, material world of darkness. Thus it visualises body as evil and world as bad.

Matter: In a material being, the substance is further sub-divided into matter and form, prime matter and substantial form to give their full names. All that we have said above, about substance applies to the substantial form of a material, embodied being. If the substantial form is the principle of *determination* (along with the accidents), making a being what it is, providing its nature and qualities, prime matter is the principle of *indetermination.* It doesn't directly contribute to what a thing is, it merely receives the relevant form. It is what, in effect, makes a being embodied, have "parts outside of parts' to use the traditional definition. It also, being the principle of indetermination, is responsible for the full realisation of the form in a particular being:

Maya: In general, maya means illusion. It also denotes the supernatural power wielded by gods and demons. It may also be regarded the power by which the universe becomes manifest; the illusion or appearance of the phenomenal world.

Meta: Meta in "metaphysics" means "after" or "beyond." The phrase *ta meta ta physika* was nothing but the collective and nondescript name given to the books of Aristotle that were placed after his treatise on Physics (Greek *meta* = after, *physika* = nature). This historical accident is not without significance for *meta* also has the connotations of "beyond" and whereas Aristotle's Physics could be summed up as a study of "nature" (the "physical" world), from the stand-point of the observable, which is the usual sand-point of the natural or physical sciences even today, metaphysics seeks to comprehend reality ("nature") at a deeper level and penetrate into its deeper depths, going beyond what mere sense-observation and experiment can reveal.

Neoesis noeseos: thought thinking about itself or "thought of thought". Aristotle discusses the *meaning* of god as being involved in self-contemplative thought ("νοήσεως νόησις (*noeseos noesis*)." According to Aristotle, the gods cannot potentially be distracted from this eternal self-contemplation because, in that instant, they would cease to exist.

Person: a rational (or, if you prefer, an intellectual) supposite. More elaborately, a person is whole, distinct, subsistent of a rational (or intellectual) nature.

Potency: see Act.

Prime Matter: See Matter.

Pulchritude: Beauty. It normally refers to physical beauty.

Res cogitans: thinking thing, which is to be contrasted with*Res extensa.* It is one of the three substances described by René Descartes in his Cartesian ontology (often referred to as "radical dualism"), alongside *res cogitans*and God. Translated from Latin, " " means "extended thing" (material thing). Descartes believed that believed that mental events belong to a distinct kind of substance — an immaterial substance.

Sat-cit-ananda. Corresponding to the Western trancendentals, Truth, Beauty and Goodness, these Indian terms mean Being, Consciousness and Bliss.

Substance: See essence.

Substantial Form: See Matter.

Substitution: the act, process, or result of substituting one thing for another. It is replacing one (set of things) with another. It is not change.

Supposite: In Thomistic *philosophy* it means a singular substance, also called suppositum, by the Scholastics, especially if the substance is a complete in itself and distinct from others.

Transcendentals: The transcendentals (Latin: transcendentalia) are the properties that every being possess by its very nature as being. Traditionally, they correspond to three aspects of the human field of interest and are their ideals; science (truth), the arts (beauty) and religion (goodness).

Transcendental Analysis: The analysis of the conditions for the possibility of direct judgement as elaborated by Joseph Maréchal is the transcendental analysis. Analysing the conditions for the possibility of direct judgement leads to Existence and Essence.

Unlimited Existence: in every human experience or encounter, we experience a limit, or the *limitation of existence*, of 'to be'. But we always tend to know more. We naturally seek for the beyond. Thus, we are tending towards the unlimited existence. Recognition of a limit means a tendency to go beyond that limit. This unlimited existence is derived from our experience of limit in every direct judgements that we experience.

Weltanschauung: A particular philosophy or view of life; the world view of an individual or group. 'Atheism is the *Weltanschauung* (comprehensive conception of the world) of persons who are free from theism - i.e., free from religion.'